Poststructuralist Readings
of the Pedagogical Encounter

D1530183

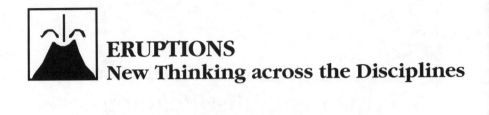

ERUPTIONS
New Thinking across the Disciplines

Erica McWilliam
General Editor

Vol. 14

PETER LANG
New York • Washington, D.C./Baltimore • Bern
Frankfurt am Main • Berlin • Brussels • Vienna • Oxford

James Palermo

Poststructuralist Readings of the Pedagogical Encounter

PETER LANG
New York • Washington, D.C./Baltimore • Bern
Frankfurt am Main • Berlin • Brussels • Vienna • Oxford

Library of Congress Cataloging-in-Publication Data

Palermo, James.
Poststructuralist readings of the pedagogical
encounter / James Palermo.
p. cm. — (Eruptions; vol. 14)
Includes bibliographical references and index.
1. Education—Philosophy. 2. Postmodernism and education.
3. Poststructuralism. I. Title. II. Series.
LB41 .P248   370'.1—dc21   00-064763
ISBN 0-8204-5211-4
ISSN 1091-8590

Die Deutsche Bibliothek-CIP-Einheitsaufnahme

Palermo, James:
Poststructuralist readings of the pedagogical
encounter / James Palermo.
–New York; Washington, D.C./Baltimore; Bern;
Frankfurt am Main; Berlin; Brussels; Vienna; Oxford: Lang.
(Eruptions; Vol. 14)
ISBN 0-8204-5211-4

Cover design by Dutton & Sherman Design
Cover photo: Augustus Saint-Gaudens, Caryatid figure (detail),
reprinted with permission of Albright-Knox Art Gallery,
Buffalo, New York, James G. Forsyth Fund, 1933

The paper in this book meets the guidelines for permanence and durability
of the Committee on Production Guidelines for Book Longevity
of the Council of Library Resources.

©2002 Peter Lang Publishing, Inc., New York

Printed in the United States of America

For Marjorie, Leslie, and Jay

Table of Contents

Acknowledgments

This book has been made possible because of the following individuals:
Michael L. Simmons, Jr.: my mentor, strategist and constant friend.
Susan D. Franzosa, who first encouraged me to do this work.
Margaret Cannizzaro and Mary K. Delmont, for their untiring textual searches.
Susan Laird and Wilma Miranda, for editorial advice, and crucial technical support from Christian Blum and Michael A. Petryshyn.
Special acknowledgment is extended to the Board of Trustees, the administration of Buffalo State College and the Department of Educational Foundations for the sabbatical semester that helped to support the writing of this manuscript.

I further acknowledge the editors of *The Philosophy of Education Yearbook* for permission to use in reedited form, material taken from the following published essays:
James Palermo. "Education, the Flesh and Aesthetic Meaning."
    Philosophy of Education, 1977, ed. Ira S. Steinberg (Urbana, Illinois: The Philosophy of Education Society, 1978).
James Palermo. "Dewey's Impossible Dream, The School and Social Progress: A Structuralist Analysis." In *Philosophy of Education*, 1985, ed. David Nyberg (Normal, Illinois: The Philosophy of Education Society, 1987), pp. 221–234.
James Palermo. "Dewey on the Pedagogy of Occupations: The Social Construction of the Hyper-Real." In *Philosophy of Education*, 1992, ed. H.A. Alexander. (Urbana, Illinois: The Philosophy of Education Society, 1993), pp. 177–190.
James Palermo. "I'm Not Lying, This Is Not a Pipe: Foucault and Magritte on the Art of Critical Pedagogy." In *Philosophy of Education*, 1994, ed. Michael S. Katz (Urbana, Illinois: The Philosophy of Education Society, 1995), pp. 192–203.
James Palermo. "Johns, Derrida, and Sartre: Reading the Metaphyics of Racism." In *Philosophy of Education*, 1998, ed. Steven Tozer (Urbana, Illinois: The Philosophy of Education Society, 1999), pp. 206–216.
James Palermo. "Reading Mann, Cubberley, and Parker on the Myth of Equal Opportunity: A Barthesian Critique." In *Philosophy of Education,* 2000. ed. Lynda Stone (Urbana, Illinois: Philosophy of Education Society, 2001), pp. 185–201.

To my mother, Kathryn, and father, Nicholas, and to my entire family, for their constant support and encouragement.

Especially to my wife, Marjorie, without whose extraordinary help and care this book would never have been completed.

Introduction:
Reading Culture and Pedagogy Using Poststructuralist Strategies

Education is an activity of social and self-formation. For the adult, this fact may be forgotten, as writing and speaking one's native tongue seems like "second nature." From the storehouse of language, the adult has chosen certain works and phrases with such regularity that an individual style emerges.

But, turning this example back to the child's acquisition of language is culture-specific. For the subject, to make his/her needs known to others, she/he must conform to language. In this sense, the subject is in language. If language is culture-specific, and the primary task of the elementary school is one of socialization, then teaching in the classroom is a political activity. And in the final instance, the teacher represents the culture, and the pedagogical encounter transmits culture to the learner on a massive scale.

This book investigates structuralist and poststructuralist thinkers, in order to discover new and critical methods of reading the pedagogical encounter. The intent is to find answers to the question, "how does pedagogy form subjectivity?" Answering this question implies answers to another question, namely, "what does it mean to be human?"

Pedagogy is used in a broad sense to include the following discursive practices: teaching, curricula, testing/classification schemes, books, and political ideologies. Reading in this context goes beyond the mechanics of decoding and encoding. Reading here presents philosophical thinkers in dialogue, i.e., ideas and methods are compared and contrasted in order to make critical sense of the politicized texts of everyday life in the school. The range of schema moves from a phenomenological description to ideology critique and deconstruction. This is a deliberate choice: poststructuralism is not "news from nowhere." The questions dealt with, and the ways in which they are couched, represent a historical continuum of inquiry. Certain issues persist, and each of the thinkers presented responds to the traces of Marxist and/or phenomenological thought, dominant in mid-twentieth century French thought.

Keeping the above in mind, the investigation is built on two premises: first, the learner is positioned as one who is constructed as a raced and gendered citizen of a certain socioeconomic class. Second, subjectivity is caught up in, and is produced by, language. Hence, the choice of poststructuralist (linguistic) philosophers: Althusser, Barthes, Baudrillard, Derrida, Foucault, Irigaray, Kristeva, Lacan, Levi-Strauss, and Merleau-Ponty. Their work has had an impact on virtually every aspect of contemporary life: art, architecture, literary criticism, feminist criticism and even popular culture itself. However, despite the impact of poststructuralism, one could argue that practitioners and their methods seem esoteric and their works somewhat misunderstood by the layperson and educationist alike. Those that mold public opinion, newspaper columnists and television political pundits, are perhaps the most obvious examples of the source of misunderstanding. A specific instance is the use of Derrida's term, *deconstruction*. In popular terms, deconstruction is seen simply as *elitist jargon,* another fashionable and arcane way of simply saying—to tear apart. But in a technically correct sense, Derrida uses the term to signify a method used to overcome metaphysical thinking. This book responds to such issues by doing several things. First, the ideas presented are placed in historical context; that is, the ideas of one thinker are traced to a preceding philosopher or issue to reveal an ongoing dialogue. Second, the ideas are located in primary sources, and a sustained effort is made to "translate" these ideas while simultaneously remaining true to the author's contextual use and intent. For example, the notion of "metaphysical thinking" not only is tied to Derrida's textual usage, but its relevance for pedagogy is also applied. An instance of the dialogue mentioned above appears in Chapter One. The issue dealt withis the existential phenomenologist Merleau-Ponty's "reading" of Cézanne's paintings. My use of this discussion is meant to present a model of a teaching encounter. Of equal importance is the reader's previewing of the historical break from phenomenology to structuralism. This is underscored as the fundamental and recurring themes of this book: embodiment, perception, and language are examined.

Each of these issues reappears in the book, but in a revised and critical expression. A further commonality in each thinker is the view that subjectivity is not unified and autonomous. Instead, the self is a historical construction of social forces and the object of conflicting ideologies. All of this impinges on and is insinuated within the pedagogical encounter itself. Thus, appealing to these thinkers is intended as a practical, critical exercise in the political reading of schooling. Everyday concerns, such as the need to evaluate the learner's cognitive development, are placed against larger cultural ideologies, such as patriarchy, racism, and social class division.

The texts examined are presented as synoptic statements of specific thinkers. This book does not presume to present an exhaustive synthesis either of the constructs or the educational applications found in the varieties of poststructuralist thought. The reader looking for a total picture or grand narrative will not find it within these pages. My task has been to deliberately avoid such "high attitude" thinking. More like a *bricoleur* or handyman, I use the materials and tools of important French thinkers on the current scene *selectively,* to unpack the school's construction of subjectivity.

The book has nine chapters. The organization moves from phenomenology, to structuralism, and finally poststructuralism, to highlight the dialogue between these thinkers. For the reader, the merit of this approach lies in the attempt to get hold of slippery concepts in their historical contexts, thereby showing the legitimacy of the educational applications that are made in this book.

Chapter One examines the existential phenomenologist, Merleau-Ponty's model of embodied meaning generation, by focusing on his essay, "Cézanne's Doubt." Merleau-Ponty's analysis of Cézanne's paintings emphasizes the observer's embodied meaning generation when seeing/reading the latter's work. What emerges is a system of equivalences or reverberation between Cézanne's strokes of pigment on canvas and imagery that the observer cocreates. This relationship is what Merleau-Ponty calls the *chaism*. The analysis fleshes out a model of the teaching encounter. Further, Merleau-Ponty's essay is pivotal because it introduces themes that are taken up and criticized by poststructuralist xiv

philosophers. Those themes include the following: 1) the presentation of autonomous subjectivity; 2) the description of the relationship of sign, image, sound, and signified, signified (idea); 3) the poststructuralist analysis of embodiment; 4) foundational thinking.

By building on Merleau-Ponty's phenomenological descriptions, Chapter Two moves to a structuralist method, placing the pedagogical encounter into a political context. The topic is the American philosopher John Dewey's essay, "The School and Social Progress." The essay concretizes Dewey's definition of education as the formation of dispositions, and demonstrates his version of cultural criticism.

Chapter Three critiques Molefi Kete Asante's program of Afrocentricity. His plan is meant to overcome the institutionalized racism of the American public school. The critique applies Althusser's Marxist/structuralist constructs of interpellation and the Ideological State Apparatus, as well as the use of Lacan's *Mirror Stage*. Placed in the context of the school, I argue that the Afrocentric subjectivity that emerges accepts *Imaginary*, alienated relationships as real.

Chapter Four uses Roland Barthes' construct of *cultural myth* to critique two important cultural ideologies that influence the formation of subjectivity. The first critique examines the American ideology of "equal educational opportunity," found in primary source texts of Horace Mann and Ellwood Cubberley, against a current assessment of schooling and "The American Dream." The second critique uncovers the mythic content of Dewey's pedagogy of history.[1]

Mann is the architect of the American Common School, while Cubberley's legacy put in place citizen models for governing the schools. The myth of the "American Dream" is that any citizen, regardless of sexual orientation, color, creed, race, or economic station has equal access to upward social mobility. Accordingly, the public school is the engine of equal opportunity for all to obtain this prize.

Barthes' reading schema examines texts at two levels. First, he presents the literal or denotative meaning of a text. At a second level of myth, or connotative meaning, Barthes reveals the politically ideological meaning of that text. The connection between Mann, Cubberley, and

[1] Citations of Dewey found throughout this book are taken from the following collection: Dewey, John, *The School and Society, The Child and the Curriculum*. Chicago, Illinois: University of Chicago Press, 1952. Themes raised in this work preview positions Dewey would develop throughout his career. Most importantly, the essays I have chosen represent talks to parents, and were meant to induce the parents to enroll their children in Dewey's University of Chicago Laboratory School.

Dewey is located in the fact that each prescribes how the child is to be formed. Barthes' constructs uncover the political implications of these positions.

Chapter Five examines one of the American schools' methods to access the child's reading readiness. The chapter applies Michel Foucault's analysis of the surrealist painter Rene Magritte's *The Treachery of Images: to critique the California Reading Readiness Test.* Magritte's painting plays on the contradiction between the realist image of a pipe and the caption below it, which denies that the representation is a pipe. Foucault treats this contradiction to show that plastic imagery need not represent something and that plastic imagery and discourse *in the same text* can be incommensurable sign systems. I place this discussion in the context of the administration of the California Reading Readiness Test given to inner city African American children whose standard usage is black English, or Eubonics. The structure, tense, and plural endings in Eubonics differs from those of Standard English. The consequence is that such children may become subjected to *normalization.* The latter, Foucault defines *politically,* as a totalizing procedure of classification and supervision used to define normality and to impose remediation and control.

Chapter Six reads a crucial element of Dewey's "New Education" as an example of what the poststructuralist Jean Baudrillard calls "Hyper-Reality." Special attention is given to the classroom simulation of occupations. This pedagogy in Baudrillard's terms is treated as a *simulacrum,* or a cultural sign system that presents an appearance or likeness as reality. Following Baudrillard's description of the dominant simulacra that characterize preindustrial, industrial, and postindustrial economies, he argues that the postmodern information society has itself emerged into a *hyper-real* world. That is to say, we are surrounded by simulacra that are without real referents in the world. I apply the *hyper-real* construct to Dewey's pedagogy of occupations. The upshot is that the occupation technique enmeshes the self in a simulation loop that is politically *Imaginary.*

Chapter Seven appeals to Jacques Derrida's reading techniques, first to expose the metaphysical foundations of racism and then to critique the American cultural pluralist model of multicultural studies as an expression of white, Anglo-Saxon Protestant capitalist ethnocentrism. The categories used are Derrida's *différance* and the *supplement.* *Différance* means both to differ in meaning and to defer meaning, as well as the impossibility of locating the absolute origin of language. *Différance* underscores the breakup of self-presence or of absolute closure in language. Appealing to commonalities with the pop artist Jasper Johns, as well as the existentialist John Paul Sartre, *différance* is used to expose racist thinking, as well as metaphysical constructs of self-presence. The next section of the chapter uses Derrida's notion of the supplement. He defines the *supplement* as an argument that appears subordinate, peripheral, or marginal. Derrida finds the *supplement* as a contrast to a keyword or *eidos*. I apply the *supplement* both to the American historian Arthur Schlesinger's book, *The Disuniting of America,* and the ideology of cultural pluralism. What is shown is the way Afro, southern, and eastern European cultures are described as supplements to the WASP hegemonic culture.

Chapter Eight examines Luce Irigaray's postfeminist critique of the ideology of male hegemony. Her focus on the political significance of the body as both a physical reality and coded discursive construct unearths reasons why women lack a voice in the symbolic order of culture.

Chapter Nine appeals to the work of the postfeminist theorist, Julia Kristeva. Her psychoanalytic/philosophical criticism of cultural patriarchy presents a different voice and new strategies for political change. Using Lacanian constructs (The Symbolic Order), as well as Barthes' notion of *jouissance* (sexual orgasm), Kristeva develops embodied meaning, particular to woman as a device of cultural critique. I use Maguerite Duras' feminist novel, *The Lover,* to expose the politically emancipatory possibilities in Kristeva's critique, in the formation of female subjectivity. This is an erotic practice of reading called *jouissance*.

Chapter 1
Merleau-Ponty: Reading Embodied Meaning and Teaching

If one looks to poststructuralist thinking in the search for a method to philosophically criticize the pedagogical encounter, where does one begin? Popularized concepts, such as *différance, jouissance,* and the *Imaginary* appear *au-courant,* but without adequate context. To orient the search, I begin with twentieth century phenomenology. The reason: *poststructuralists reject, amend, and incorporate constructs taken from the phenomenologists*: Husserl, Heidegger, Sartre, and Merleau-Ponty. In this framework, Maurice Merleau-Ponty is the transitional figure. He was a colleague of both the existential phenomenologist Jean Paul Sartre and structuralist Claude Levi-Strauss. With Sartre, Merleau-Ponty's connection is the shared issues of freedom, political engagement, and the body. With Levi-Strauss, the direction moves to language.

The discussion below will focus on Merleau-Ponty's central concerns of the relationship between perception, meaning generation, and the body as it is lived.

To orient my reading of Merleau-Ponty, a summary statement of

Husserl's phenomenological enterprise follows. Husserl's task was to find a foundation to ground the truth of the special sciences. He took as his model the laws of logic. An example is the logical law of non-contradiction. Such a logical law, (as distinct from a logical rule), governs any psychological experience of finding and speaking the truth. Such a law was true for Aristotle and will remain true for humankind in the future. Husserl reasoned that such a phenomenon must be correlative to the structure of consciousness itself. Hence, his term *phenomenology,* or the study of appearing reality, i.e., reality as it appears to consciousness.

The search for the bedrock *origins* of knowledge meant a search for ideas or essences. One example of an essence is the *Kreutzer Sonata*; this musical score, played now, one hundred years ago, or a century from now, remains unchanged. The score remains identical, irreal (not confined to the here and now), and a-temporal, despite innumerable physical performances of the piece.

Key in this search was Husserl's description of consciousness as always being consciousness of something. In his words, *consciousness* is *intentional* or directed outward, toward some "object." What that object is for consciousness depends on the mode in which it is intended. For example, as I write I *perceive* this yellow sheet before me, I can *remember* it tomorrow, *calculate* its dimensions, and *imagine* its other possible uses. I can even invest the sheet with *emotional* significance, thinking of it as the location of my work. Out of this movement, the existential-phenomenologist equates consciousness with human *freedom.* In this connection, Husserl's description of *internal time consciousness* describes consciousness fundamentally as a temporal phenomenon. Objects appearing to consciousness are experienced in a "specious present." The "present" is not composed of discrete instants, but instead appears with overlapping halos of the past both immediate and more distant, together with the anticipations of the near and more distant future. All of this recurs *modified,* in Heidegger's *Being and Time*, and in Derrida's central construct of *différance.*[1] For the existential-phenomenologist, the temporal dimension of consciousness delivers an

---

[1] Against Husserl's emphasis on the present, Heidegger's ontological descriptions emphasized the propulsive future character of temporal experience.

autonomous subject whose choices overcome an all-determining past. Sartre's notion of the transcendence of the ego is an example. On the other hand, the poststructuralist Derrida faults Husserl for failing to grasp the separations of absence and presence within temporality. More on this follows the Derrida chapter.

Each of the phenomenologists mentioned—Heidegger, Sartre, and Merleau-Ponty—*rejected* Husserl's epistemological search for essences. But they retained his description of the intentionality of consciousness, turning the course of phenomenology in a new direction. That direction was ontological: toward a study of the meaning of Being, focusing on the human subject, more properly described as "being in the world."

A crucial issue appearing first in Husserl's *Formal and Transcendental Logic* and later in his *Krisis* book, concerns the relationship between the lived-body and meaning generation.

This issue is the centerpiece of Merleau-Ponty's phenomenological investigations. It is here that I take up his examination of the connections between the lived-body, perception, *original meaning generation,* and the aesthetic object as a paradigm of the pedagogical encounter, as well as Merleau-Ponty's description of the child's acquisition of language.

These connections are laid out in Merleau-Ponty's essay, "Cézanne's Doubt."[2] The core argument is that aesthetic meaning is not predicative, i.e., it does not take the discursive form "S is P." Obviously, a positivist reading would claim that the aesthetic object lacks a "verification principle," not only with respect to its referents, but even as to its communicability."[3]

Merleau-Ponty rejects this position. He argues that the meaning of an aesthetic object is uncovered in concentrated attention to our embodiment.[4] This means that (1) the aesthetic object does express meanings, (2) the connection between the artist's creative activity, his/her product, the aesthetic object, and the observer's active reception

---

[2] Maurice Merleau-Ponty, "Cézanne's Doubt." trans. Hubert L. Dreyfus and Patricia Allen Dreyfus in *Sense and Non-Sense*, ed. Wild (Evanston: Northwestern University Press, 1964), 12.

[3] See, for example, Morris Weltz, "The Role of Theory in Aesthetics," *Journal of Aesthetics and Art Criticism* 15 (1956): 27–35.

[4] I have drawn this theme from Louis Arnaud Reid, "Education and Aesthetic Meaning," *British Journal of Aesthetics* 26 (1973): 271–284.

4

of the aesthetic object is dialogical, (3) aesthetic meaning represents the lived-body's pre-predicative perceptual significations, i.e., significations which undergird the formulation of predicative judgments, (4) the aesthetic task is to make the invisible, visible and (5) understanding aesthetic meaning is educationally crucial because it expresses a phenomenological *style* for the teaching-learning process. The argument is drawn from his discussion of Cézanne's attempt to recover the lived unfolding of the perceptual spectacle. The problem is to describe how the "lived-body's" insertion into the world represents a *chiasm*, which is Merleau-Ponty's description of the crossover intrinsic to the act of perception.[5] That is, in perceiving something, what we see is performed or constituted by our sensing body and at the same time the product of a process that we undergo. The chiasm represents the shift of meaning intrinsic to the dialogue between teacher and student, artist and observer, incarnate human and world.

Remembering that consciousness is always directed toward some object, the genesis of intentional objects is what Husserl referred to as the doing or act character of consciousness.[6] This does not mean that phenomenologists limit the sense making of consciousness to judgmental or predicative activity. Rather, the investigation of intentional activity begins with *the most original modality of consciousness,* the act of perception. Moreover, perceptual meanings are not the sort that can be stated in propositional form. Instead, the act of perception generates nondiscursive meanings that are constituted corporeally in the lived world. The "world" in this sense is the dialectical field of a *subject* who first lives or embodies meanings before these meanings are fully understood. The world as it is lived discloses itself through a theme-horizon relationship, while the world, at its primordial level, is an all encompassing pre-understood ground which we are given over to and bound to directly by the immediate experience of situations.[7] This world horizon is not an object of experience but an implicit awareness, i.e., a

---

5   Maurice Merleau-Ponty, *The Visible and the Invisible,* trans. A. Lingis (Evanston: Northwestern University Press, 1968), 123.

6   Edmund Husserl, *Ideas: General Introduction to Pure Phenomenology,* trans. W.R. Boyce Gibson (New York: Macmillan Company, 1962), 333.

7   Gerd Brand, "The Structure of the Life World According to Husserl," *Man and World*: 6 (May 1973) 144.

silent and essentially perceptual structure of experience.

Therefore, the phenomenology of perception is the explication of the sensory data which are "passively synthesized" in a bodily founded context.[8] Passively synthesized or embodied meanings derive from neither blind reflexes nor cognitive judgments; they occupy a mean between both operations. The simple perceptions of routine experience validate what can be termed this motive power of the body.[9] The ordinary activity of moving about in one's apartment is an example. Entering my study, I am in the habit of moving my eyes toward the left, focusing them on my bookshelf. Today, as I move my eyes toward the left, I notice the visual spectacle also seems to move to the left. In fact, I am aware of the instant in which the side-slip of my eyes' movement and the fixing of my new view (the bookshelf) come together. On the other hand, ". . . at no moment do I know that the images remain stationary on the retina."[10] But even more importantly, I never suffer from the ultimate confusion of believing that the room is actually moving to the left. Merleau-Ponty accounts for this by saying that movements of the body are invested with perceptual significance. Thus, the illusion of the room's movement is recognized as an illusion because it is " . . . 'accounted for' by the movement of the organs of perception. The body provides the 'motive for changes in the spectacle.'"[11] My gaze and the bookshelf remain stuck together. Such a pre-predicative consciousness recovers the immanent meaning of a "lived through" logic which is distinct from intellectual activities, such as reflection. The awareness that the room is not moving is neither learned nor deduced. This is what Merleau-Ponty calls body-intentionality.

Merleau-Ponty has used Gestaltist terminology to describe these embodied perceptual meanings. A brief consideration of his schema is crucial because I want to show how the meaning embodied symbol works in the aesthetic dialogue between artist and viewer, teacher and student. Consider the figure-ground relationship that ushers in that shift of consciousness necessary both to learning and to the aesthetic attitude,

[8] Edmund Husserl, *Experience and Judgment,* trans. J.J. Churchill and K. Ameriks (Evanston: Northwestern University Press), 257.
[9] Merleau-Ponty, *Phenomenology of Perception,* 50.
[10] Ibid., 48
[11] Ibid.

6

namely, "attention." Merleau-Ponty says:

> . . . to pay attention is not merely further to elucidate pre-existing data, it is to bring about a new articulation of them by taking them as figures. They are preformed only as horizons, they constitute in reality new regions in the total world. It is precisely the original structure which they introduce that brings out the identity of the object before and after the act of attention.[12]

This shift of consciousness is what underwrites all learning. Attention reestablishes the unity of an object in a new dimension. Attention is the active constitution of a new object, making explicit what was previously implicit. More concretely, "attention" shifts the observer's perception of splotches of color painted on a canvas into a coherent figure. Attention shifts the learner's perception of swiggly lines on a sheet of paper into letters which form words. Obviously, securing the attention of his audience is the necessary first step in the artist's aesthetic dialogue. Husserl puts the issue of attention forward in his description of the aesthetic attitude at work in the apprehension of Durer's engraving, "The Knight, Death and the Devil." He describes the shift of consciousness intrinsic to the aesthetic observation of Durer's engraving as a neutralization of the data of ordinary perception. In the aesthetic attitude, one moves away from the objects of normal perception to the depicted realities contained within the engraving. Thus, the same physical things—lines engraved on paper but apprehended in the aesthetic attitude—stand out in pictorial "flesh and blood" as "The Knight, Death and the Devil." In sum, aesthetic meaning emerges out of a certain *form* or *style* of seeing which imposes itself on us through our active participation.

A *style* can be detected in the aesthetic object by the way in which certain figures are repeated to the neglect of other possible figures implicit within the work. To return to the Gestaltist language, one understands an artist's style, "seeing" the object or work of art in a holistic way, i.e., by transforming the sensory data into the larger meaning which transcends the literal or specific. The chiasm or crossover echoed in the aesthetic object—the reversibility, which makes the art-symbol communicable—is located in the form schema of perception as it

---

[12]   Ibid., 30.

is lived. This means that I do not see patches of color. I see objects that are colored. Further, it means that even though certain parts of the retina are blind to blue or red, on looking at a blue or a red surface I do not see any discolored areas. "My perception is not limited to what the retinal stimuli prescribe, but reorganizes these stimuli so as to establish the field's homogeneity."[13]

Likewise, things heard become meaningful because they are apprehended as figures having a dialectical relationship to the whole. In listening to a song, the coherence of its melody derives not from the summation of individual notes, but from their structural function. The work of jazz pianist Theolonius Monk demonstrates that the repeated coherent distortion of musical phrases allows the whole melody to remain intact. More importantly, the holistic intelligibility of perception represents the synergy of my body's being. I do not possess five separate and discrete senses that translate separate and discrete visual, tactile, and audible information. Instead, ". . . I grasp a unique structure of the thing, a unique way of being which speaks to all of my senses at once."[14] This is the body's *form* structure of synesthesia; the activity of one sense modality which interprets or suggests the data of another sense modality. It is this intersensory coordination which accounts for the synthesis of the body image and lies at the heart of embodied meaning. Perception then is not the rudimentary form of intelligence, nor is the generation of meaning dependent on the intervention of intelligence or judgment. Consciousness has a correlate in the body that is neither predicative nor physiological, but represents the synthesis of both: body intentionality. The point is that the classical distinction between mind and body, together with the methods of introspection of inner psychic states or its opposite, the observation of outer physical responses, falls apart.

The significance of this for understanding the aesthetic symbol is curious. Merleau-Ponty leaves phenomenology momentarily by comparing the expression of emotions to language, employing the structuralist model of language using the terms of sign-signified. He argues that both the word and the emotion expressed have an immanent signification, whose meaning is expressed directly in their signs. To say

---

[13]   Ibid., 48.
[14]   Ibid., 50.

8

that the word and the gesture (or spoken word) have an immanent meaning is to say that the speaker and his partner share a sedimented use of patterns which allow the body to express its world and its emotions. Words, therefore, are neither artificial nor natural signs, but the dialectical synthesis of both. Simply because humans have the same kinds of emotions and have the same kinds of organs does not mean that they produce the same kinds of signs. Merleau-Ponty cites the Japanese, who smiles when he is angry and the Westerner, whose anger is revealed by going red, stamping his feet, and hissing his words. ". . . What is important is how they use their bodies, the simultaneous patterning of body and world in emotion."[15]

The conclusion: the meaning of behavior is shown by its expression: meaning adheres to behavior.

> . . . Anger, shame, hate and love are not psychic facts hidden at the bottom of another's consciousness: they are types of behavior or styles of conduct that are visible from the outside. They exist in this fact, or in those gestures not hidden behind them.[16]

For Merleau-Ponty, the comparison between linguistic meaning and aesthetic meaning is valid because words bear meaning in the same way that the body incarnates a manner of behavior. For him, the comparison rests on the view that the artist's painting or playing is a sensory equivalent that represents the meanings of his body as it is lived. Once again the crux of the argument is that the possession of speech is correlative to the manner in which one possesses the body: ". . . the main areas of my body are devoted to actions and participate in their value. I move my legs not as things in space two and one-half feet from my head but as a power of locomotion which extends my motor intention downward."[17]

When I move myself, at no time do I have to conjure up a representation of my movement before I move. My movement in space is accomplished by my actual movement. This same paradigm is applicable to human speech. All of this falls into place once we understand what a

---

[15] Ibid., 189.
[16] Ibid.
[17] Ibid., 146.

word is and what it means to have a word. When I have a word, ". . . I possess its articulatory and acoustic style as one of the modulations, one of the possible uses of my body."[18] Whenever I want to use a word, ". . . I reach back for it as my hand reaches towards the part of my body which is being pricked; the word has a certain location in my linguistic world, and is part of my equipment."[19]

Throughout, Merleau-Ponty privileges the spoken word over the written word. If speaking is a conversion of my body intentionality into vocal form, in neither act does the subject submit to a representation of the movement before it is accomplished. In a normal situation, the speaker does not puzzle out the "correct" combinations of words before he uses them. This is why the act of speaking can be compared to the artistic performance: "I have only one means of representing it (the word) which is uttering it, just as the artist has only one means of representing the work in which he is engaged: by doing it."[20]

Words and thoughts are self-referential. They are accomplished in and with the expression, itself. In its ultimate sense, the word is thought's body. As in the aesthetic performance, *speech* has ". . . the unique capacity to express expressions and to express itself."[21]

In Merleau-Ponty's terms, the marriage of linguistic meaning and expression, sign and signification, is one of *style*, which presents again that "sense" is made incarnate through the body, i.e., the word is a linguistic concept that has an affective value as existential mimicry rather than as a conceptual statement. Merleau-Ponty describes this *style* as ". . . *a central inner experience, specifically verbal thanks to which the sound heard, uttered, read, or written becomes a linguistic fact and the word carries the thought.*"[22]

For Merleau-Ponty, in understanding the function of *style* in speech, we can come to see the connection between the aesthetic performance and speech. In both, the meaning swallows up the sign. Put differently, there exists in both the *spoken word* and the aesthetic performance a

---

18   Ibid., 180.
19   Ibid.
20   Ibid.
21   Jacques Ehrmann, ed., *Structuralism* (Garden City: Doubleday & Co., Inc., 1970), 17.
22   Merleau-Ponty, *Phenomenology of Perception,* 182.

radical inseparability between meaning and expression. This theme returns to the central connection between learning and the aesthetic attitude, namely, the shift of consciousness that we have called attention. Merleau-Ponty cites his proof in the actress La Berma's portrayal of Phaedra and Proust's analysis of "La Sonate de Vinteuil."[23] On stage, La Berma is no longer a person but the persona, herself. Analogously, in the intellectual analysis of the sonata we must always revert to our actual experience of hearing it. What we find is that the notes of the sonata, like La Berma's portrayal of Phaedra, are not its signs, but its vehicle and its meaning. The sign and the signified are self-referential; their meaning is accomplished in and with the expression, itself. But the radical inseparability of these phenomena underscore the deeper unity which we heard Husserl speak of before—that is, the oneness of the act of attention and the constitution of a new understanding of the world.

But this is only one side of the issue. To know something oneself and to describe this knowledge to another by engaging that person in dialogue is not to guarantee that your meaning is understood. Taken a further step, in teaching, as in aesthetic expression, the problem is not simply in the telling but in the showing. Merleau-Ponty takes up the problem of showing how meaning is generated in his investigation of Cézanne. Merleau-Ponty's central theme is that the joy of art lies in its showing how the perceptual act takes on meaning, how the objects in space take on solidity. But this joy is nothing other than the artist's problem and the source of his doubt. For Cézanne, the problem demanded his elaboration of a *system of equivalences,* i.e., a means to catch the diffused meanings of his perceptual experience and to give them a separate existence in the work, itself. But whether or not the artist can bring all of this off in large part depends on a partner, the viewer. The viewer identifies the diffused meanings that the artist has caught only if the aesthetic object calls forth the viewer's *system of equivalences:* the viewer must be able to reconstitute his/her own perceptual experience. Very simply, Cézanne's *style:* the manner in which he accomplishes his goal, the movement of his hands, his choice of colors must present anew the meanings of perception. He must articulate new figures previously submerged in the perceptual horizon.

---

[23]   Ibid., 183.

He must endow the sensible with meaning. Paraphrasing Merleau-Ponty, the painter must recover the routine achievement of visual perception hidden in everyday experience and explicate our silent handling of a world which we "people" with objects. If the invisible organization of the perceptual spectacle is to be made visible we must "see and re-enact it." Cézanne's problem is pedagogical, i.e., his work must show the viewer how they both constitute the visibility of things seen. And to say that art shares the naming function of language is not hyperbole. Words name by taking up the inchoate appearance of things, placing them before us, and making them recognizable. But, ". . . words do not look like the things they designate; and a picture is not a *trompe-l'oeil*."[24]

Merleau-Ponty says that Cézanne's doubt lies in the artist's concern about his ability to create an image that takes on life for others. Specifically for Cézanne, the ready-made formula of pointillism was rejected because the break-up of tones submerged the pictorial object by robbing it of weight. On the other hand, the prefabricated Renaissance rendering of three-dimensional geometric space falsified the live spectacle.[25] ". . . For example, to say that a circle seen obliquely is seen as an ellipse is to substitute for our actual perception what we would see if we were cameras: in reality we see a *form* which oscillates around the ellipse without being an ellipse."[26]

Merleau-Ponty tells us that Cézanne's answer is to paint what are apparent perceptual violations. In a portrait of Mme. Cézanne, the background border of wallpaper does not mesh with the boundaries of her body. In the painting of Gustave Geoffrey, a large table stretches at the bottom so that, ". . . when our eye runs over a large surface, the images it successfully receives are taken from different points of view, and the whole surface is warped."[27]

On one level, this comes close to the meaning of Cézanne's aesthetic dialogue. Cézanne's paintings speak because they represent the *style* of the body's synergy: shape, depth, sight, and touch are intertwined in his use of coloration. Their technique cannot depend on outline because an outline presents shape but with loss of depth. The outlined object appears

---

[24] Merleau-Ponty, *Sense and Non-Sense,* 17.
[25] Ibid., 12.
[26] Ibid., 14.
[27] Ibid.

12

as a two-dimensional appendage having neither back nor sides. On the other hand, ". . . not to indicate any shape would be to deprive the objects of their identity."[28] To represent objects as they swell before us, Cézanne distorts perspective variations and combines them in several blue outlines. The result is that, "our vision rebounds among these outlines, perspectival distortions come together, and a new figure takes form, the object appears organizing itself before our eyes."[29] The generation of meaning results from the artist's reversion to his body's system of equivalences: the centering of his attention on his own gesture and the extension of that gesture in his work.[30] On a more universal level, the ordering or execution itself is what defines the thought. This is a substitution of equivalent meanings, of lived perceptual experience and bodily gestures, that transform those meanings.[31] The artist must make the outside and inside vision decipherable by the body and sense must articulate the thought. But, vision is attached to movement. We see what we look at. What would vision be without eye movement?

> Everything I see is in principle within my reach, at least within reach of my sight and is marked on the map of the "I can" [move my body]. My movement is not a decision made by the mind, a *style* of language. The *style* is defined neither by words nor by ideas. It possesses not a direct signification, but an oblique one."[32]

This, of course, is what we have meant by the chiasm or crisscrossing of body and meaning in the perceptual act, in speaking, and in the creation of the aesthetic object. Human and world, speaker and listener, artist and viewer are the embodiment of the human *style* of being in the world.

In the remainder of this chapter, I want to explicate those aspects of *style* secreted between the lines of Merleau-Ponty's aesthetic in order to show how the generation of aesthetic meaning stands as a remarkable

---

28 Ibid., 15.
29 Merleau-Ponty, *Phenomenology of Perception*, 100.
30 Ibid., 50.
31 Walter J. Bate, *Major British Writers* (New York: Harcourt, Brace and Co., 1954), 258, citing John Keats.
32 Maurice Merleau-Ponty, *Consciousness and the Acquisition of Language,* trans. Hugh J. Silverman (Evanstown: Northwestern University Press, 1973), 31.

insight into the pedagogical dialogue. The pervasive theme throughout Merleau-Ponty's aesthetic is that meaning is expressed in a practical and Gestalt structure. The body takes up the lived situation, and originates a practical relationship between its tasks, itself, and external space. The body is always tacitly understood in the figure-ground relationship as an invariant core of meaning. The action of moving my hand toward my pen is illustrative of this direct projection of me toward an object of the world.

That is, each movement of my hand recapitulates the preceding movements of my hand's activity directed toward the goal of picking up the pen. I do not deduce the location of the pen and then "program" my own movements. Rather all of this is immediate: it flows from my capacity for motor differentiation within the dynamic body image.

Merleau-Ponty designates this body integration at work in perception as the prepredicative foundation for the higher cognitive activity of the categorical attitude. The categorical attitude is the problem solving power that finds the *form* or *style* of a present situation projected into future situations. Originally, the categorical attitude shows itself as the body's *synesthesia:* "...a system of equivalences, immediately given invariant whereby the different motor tasks are instantaneously transferable."[33]

As a consequence of this, the problem of meaning generation is seen as having two dialectical poles, the one is epistemological, while the other is practical. On the epistemological side, the teacher asks himself, "How will my student best understand the ideas that I present?" On the practical side one must ask, "What kind of activities must be performed if these concepts are to become relevant to the student's lived experience?" Thus, in a real sense, the problem of the teacher is the analogue of Cézanne's aesthetic problem. Cézanne's *re-presentation* of lived space is entwined within the geometry teacher's attempt to represent the meaning of a triangle as a three-dimensional figure in space having three angles, the sum of which are equal to two right angles. Like the observer's understanding of Cézanne's paintings, the student's understanding of the geometrical definition of a triangle is not an analytic necessity, nor does it involve the student's intuition of the

---

[33] Merleau-Ponty. *Phenomenology of Perception*, p. 41.

14

Cézanne, Paul. "Madame Cézanne Seated." 1893-1894. Private collection.

essence of triangularity. Instead, understanding the meaning of a triangle is originally comparable to understanding the "meaning" of Cézanne's paintings. The learner first must incarnate the geometric figure: measurement of space is a reordering of perceptual experience. The learner must move his/her body and draw the idea on paper. One first understands the angles of the triangle not as "objective things," but as movements which orient him/her into a system of possible bodily movements. As in the aesthetic attitude, the lines that the student draws do not appear as simple lines of a figure, but as lines of force. The necessity of the student's understanding that the triangle has angles, the sum of which equals two right angles, is made possible because of "... the experience of a real triangle, and because he knows that as a physical thing the triangle displays all of the possibilities it can ever show."[34] In the above, the point has been not to describe a radical new departure in teaching, but to reveal the truth of those incarnate meanings that are taken for granted.

In summary, Merleau-Ponty argues that aesthetic meaning is real, communicable, and has its origins in embodiment: a union exists between aesthetic and linguistic meaning in the syntax of the flesh. Indeed, the problem of aesthetic meaning makes visible not the telling but the showing of meanings. In both, Merleau-Ponty's examples of the

---

[34]   Ibid., 388.

artist and my own of the teacher, the viewer and the student are shown how to name their own experience by the multiplying of their own flesh's system of equivalencies. It is in this way that the chiasm is made real: perception is reversed; the invisible is made visible and "what is inside is also outside."

At the outset, I claimed that Merleau-Ponty is a transitional figure between phenomenology and structuralism. Evidence for this assertion was found in the "Cézanne's Doubt" essay above, in which he uses the structuralist terminology *sign* and *signified,* to describe the creative activity of aesthetic experience. Throughout, linguistic expression and communication are joined to the body's *gestural schema,* which is correlative to speaking. This previews Merleau-Ponty's last investigation, in which language takes primacy over perception.

But, two questions become salient. First, where does Merleau-Ponty's shift toward structuralism begin? Second, is his use of structuralist motifs "correct" or a misreading?

One source of Merleau-Ponty's affinity for structuralism is located in his use of the term *form,* which is synonymous in his usage with structure. Structure (as already seen) has a Gestaltist figure/ground, or theme/horizon composition. A structural/phenomenological description replaces atomistic *partes extra partes* analysis, in favor of a holistic view in which the whole is greater than the sum of its parts. *This is not the Sausserian structure that begins with the sign structure of language, but the phenomenological data of pre-linguistic consciousness.* Here, a brief consideration of Merleau-Ponty's reading of Saussure previews issues raised in the paradigm shift of structuralism.

Merleau-Ponty's reading of Saussure is controversial on several scores. First, Merleau-Ponty emphasizes the *sign-signified* relationship. *The integral relation of signifier, signified sign* is passed over; moreover, his notion that words have *immanent signification* will be shown to be problematic.

Merleau-Ponty's misreading of other structuralists is also controversial. His reading of Claude Levi-Strauss fails to take into account the latter's explicit rejection both of the phenomenological apparatus, and especially the deterministic view of the subject.

But perhaps most dramatic is Merleau-Ponty's misreading of Jacques Lacan on the child's psychosexual development. In his essay, "The

16

Child's Relation With Others," Merleau-Ponty repeats the description of the body's synethesia by putting it into a Lacanian format.[35] That is, the child's acquisition of language is predicated on his overcoming the egocentric predicament: the child realizes that not only does he see a visual spectacle, his body is part of the other's own visual spectacle. Put differently, his/her behavior is mirrored by others who respond to that behavior. Following Lacan, there is a shift from the *lived-body* to the *specular body* in the child's acquisition of language.

Now, Merleau-Ponty says this process integrates both the child's imagination and the real. The upshot is the child's identification with others, which will inaugurate the possibility of a *superego*.

This reading of Lacan is problematic: Merleau-Ponty ascribes ordinary usage to the terms *imaginary* and *real,* neglecting Lacan's specialized terminology. Consequently, Merleau-Ponty distorts the *imaginary* phase of development (to be described in Chapter Two). For Lacan, the *imaginary* is the site of the ego, not the superego.

Having said that, the issues that Merleau-Ponty raises—subjectivity and freedom, perception and the gaze, the body, the work of language, and the *chiasm*—have had an enduring resonance for structuralist and poststructuralist thinkers alike. Moreover, it is the interconnection between the specular body, language, and cultural myth that are key to an understanding of the school's formation of subjectivity.

Chapter Two moves to a structuralist model, and develops the construct of the specular self, which continues the investigation of the formation of subjectivity in the school, with a combined Levi-Straussian and Lacanian reading of "Dewey's School and Social Progress."

---

[35] For Merleau-Ponty's reading of Jacques Lacan on the child's acquisition of language, see "The Child's Relations With Others," trans. William Cobb in *The Primacy of Perception and Other Essays* (Evanston: Northwestern University Press, 1964), 96–155.

Chapter 2
Lacan:
Reading Dewey
as Dreamwork

John Dewey occupies a central place in the pantheon of Western philosophy. His brand of American pragmatism (which he called instrumentalism) had a worldwide impact. As a champion of democracy, he insisted that democracy must be actualized as a form of "conjoint living." In his vision, the school is the place where democracy is experienced.

The following encapsulates his demand that the educative process be one of inculcating specific habits toward the end of democratic living:

> If we are willing to conceive education as the process of forming dispositions intellectual and emotional toward nature and fellow man, philosophy may even be defined as the general theory of education.[1]

These words, taken from John Dewey's text, *Democracy and Education,* succinctly describe his conflation of the activities of philosophy and education. Dewey himself would find it a bitter irony that his ideas and methods have not been used in the construction of a new social order.

---

[1]   John Dewey, *Democracy and Education* (New York: The Free Press, 1966), 328.

18

Instead, his works appear to have been domesticated as pallid homilies that enunciate the American dogma of efficient problem solving. Obviously, such an analysis is too simplistic. Nonetheless, I believe that an assessment of Dewey's work coincides with his own goal—that is, of making the philosophical activity of social critique. But, such a task demands nothing less than the exposure of the ideological seams of the Deweyan corpus itself. The point here is not to attack Dewey. Instead, my aim in this chapter is two-pronged: (1) introduce both Claude Levi-Strauss and Jacques Lacan's structuralist technique of criticism, and (2) apply these techniques to a specific text—Dewey's "The School and Social Progress."

The structuralist technique is archeological. Therefore, Dewey's text will not be read in a straightforward manner. Instead, appealing to the structuralist Claude Levi-Strauss, I shall begin my reading of the essay as a cultural myth. The implications are threefold. The first implication is metaphysical. Levi-Strauss jettisons the phenomenological investigation of consciousness and its corollary of human freedom. He argues that meaning is not founded in the subject's lived experience, but resides in signs that are organized as cultural structures. The second implication is methodological, while the third is definitional. Methodologically, to read Dewey's essay as a cultural myth means that what is written shall not be taken at face value. Instead, my reading tries to "reconstruct the system of concepts behind the words. The aim is to discover the undiscovered, by recovering what is latent in the text."[2] The recovery of these latent meanings exposes Dewey's problematic or conceptual framework. Such an exposure tells us what counts as relevant data. Further, it spells out the forms and conditions within which problems can be posed for Dewey. Levi-Strauss takes "cultural myth" to mean the following:

(a) The myth is the culturally sanctioned ground for understanding the world. The mythic ground functions to provide the individual with answers for cultural contradictions and dilemmas.
(b) The myth has a narrative with a didactic, moral, and therapeutic message.
(c) The myth is an internally coherent sign system. The function of a sign is to represent that which is absent.

---

[2] Claude Levi-Strauss, *Structural Anthropology*, trans.Basic Books, New York, 1963. See also Miriam Glucksman, *Structuralist Analysis in Contemporary Social Thought* (London: Routledge & Kegan Paul, 1974), 4.

(d) Decoding the myth's sign system reveals meaning
    absent from conscious experience and repressed.[3]

Levi-Strauss decodes the repressed meanings in cultural myths by integrating the methods of Freudian dreamwork and linguistic structuralism. His *Elementary Structures of Kinship* reveals a hidden structure that is beneath all universal or crosscultural lived experience, i.e., the Oedipus Complex becomes that core structure which subtends the sociocultural organization of society. My own analysis of Dewey's essay is not so bold, but it will get at "The School and Social Progress" by using dreamwork and structuralist archeological techniques. Continuing the above methodological description, here I want to sketch structuralist techniques, then I shall consider the outlines of a Lacanian revision of Freud's dream interpretation. Finally, I shall integrate the two methods as a preparation for the analysis of the Dewey text.

The structuralist paradigm originates with the linguist Ferdinand Saussure, whose original discovery was that the meaning of a *linguistic sign* is secreted between two elements: the *signifier,* or articulated expression, and the *signified,* or articulated concept. Linguistic meanings then must be seen as dialectical structures: any change in a single element simultaneously changes the entire constellation of elements. On the other hand, the meaning of a sign system derives from the continuities that exist among and between signifiers. Modern structuralism represents both an assimilation and extension of this semiotic paradigm into the disciplines of anthropology, literary criticism, philosophy, and psychoanalysis. The structuralist interface between these disciplines is in the work of revealing the hidden tracery of self to culture, self to other, and self to self, by rejoining the lost connection between cultural signs.

Paul Ricoeur condenses the activity of structuralist analysis into four moves: First, "work on a closed corpus; second, . . . establish inventories of elements; third, . . . place these elements in relations of opposition; fourth, . . . establish a calculus of possible combinations." The union of these structuralist techniques and Freudian dreamwork is set down by the psychoanalyst Jacques Lacan. Lacan argues that the unconscious is structured like language and that the hidden connections between consciousness and the unconscious can be deciphered by piecing

---

[3]   Eugen Bar, "Myth and Primary Process: A Psychoanalytic Approach," *Ars Semeiotica* (May 1955): pp. 101–108. The mythic component of this study is modeled on Bar's perspicacious reading of Freudian "dreamwork."

together the symbols appearing in dreams. Dreamwork involves deciphering and then integrating the symbolism of the two interdependent texts of human experience. The one text, that of waking experience or *consciousness,* is both phylogenetically and ontogenetically derivative in the sense that it is founded on a more primary process of thinking. The unconscious and the dream represent examples of that primary process. Freud describes the dream as the vehicle of repression. That is to say, the unconscious entertains desires that are explicitly proscribed by the culture. This proscription may be so fundamental, and consequently so overwhelming to the psyche, that the psyche prevents the proscribed libidinous object from appearing to consciousness. Freud calls this repression. Now, since the individual is not free to release libidinous energy on his real object of desire, he must find a substitute object. Freud sees the topological space of the dream as the answer. In the dream, libidinous energy is displaced onto a substitute object. In Lacan's linguistic structuralist terms, the libidinous energy is displaced onto a signifier that stands for, takes the place of, and marks the absence of the real object of desire.

Repression works in the dream through the linguistic device of metaphor, where one term is substituted for another on the basis of similarity. "He is a shark" is a linguistic example of metaphor. In the dream the link between unconscious, forbidden libidinous object, and the cultural reality is overcome. The repressed object takes the status of a signifier in the dream. In structuralist terms, the dream signifier becomes the metaphoric equivalent of the repressed object of desire. The upshot is that the dreamer has it both ways at once. On the one hand, the dream fulfills the dreamer's desire for the forbidden, repressed object. On the other hand, the repressed object appears under the disguise of metaphoric signifier. This disguise allows the dreamer possession of the repressed object while simultaneously allowing him to semiotically deny that the fulfillment of his desire is being accomplished. Thus, the dream signifier represents the absence of what is repressed. Through the dream, the signifier reclaims the absent desire of waking life. In the dream, the real cultural world, or, its prohibitions, is inverted; the interdict of repressed desire is reversed. The impossible dream is realized because the latent meaning of the signifier is separated from consciousness, while the manifest meaning of the signifier is separated from the unconscious.

The goal of Lacanian dreamwork then, is to reveal the repressed but contiguous relationship of the metonymic and metaphoric signifiers to the culturally acceptable inversion. That is, the analyst must work to piece together both the latent and manifest meanings of the dream's symbols. This is done by reading between the lines of the dream's grammar.[4]

The above analysis has described the analogous relationship of cultural myth and dream, together with a structuralist method for deciphering both. Throughout, the larger concern has been to specify a method to be used in unpacking the repressive function of a specific cultural myth, namely Dewey's essay, "The School and Social Progress."[5]

The analysis begins with the major thematic of Dewey's essay. Because "The School and Social Progress" is treated as a myth, the next move will be the search for "mythemes," or bundles of relations that share a common trait within the essay. The purpose of this search is to expose the corpus which shapes the myth. The conjunction of these oppositions will locate the problematic within Dewey's model. Finally, the repressive ideology of the essay will be considered.

Bernstein quite accurately describes the cultural contradiction which Dewey addressed in his essay as alienation, i.e., Dewey believed "economic and political institutions can without controlled direction create an alienated society that undermines that direct sharing, face-to-face communication, and individual responsibility required for effective democracy."[6] Early on, Dewey raises the alienation issue with the rhetorical question, "can we connect this 'New Education' with the general march of events?"[7] Later in the essay, he muses about Plato. Without using the term "alienation," that is clearly what he has in mind:

> Plato somewhere speaks of the slave as one who in his actions does not express his own ideas, but those of some other man. [Dewey goes on to say that our social problem now is even more urgent than in the time of Plato. That method, purpose, and understanding shall exist in the consciousness of the one who does the work, that his activity shall have meaning to himself.[8]

---

[4]   In a real sense, Lacan is not strictly a structuralist. Although he retains Saussure's model, it becomes radicalized. That is, signifiers refer to other signifiers; context changes the meaning of signifiers, which themselves may not have a referent in the world.

[5]   Richard J. Bernstein, *John Dewey* (New York: Washington Square Press, Inc., 1967), 139.

[6]   John Dewey, "The School and Social Progress," in *The Child and the Curriculum and the School and Society* (Chicago: The University of Chicago Press, 1971), 8.

[7]   Ibid. 23.

[8]   Fritz Pappenheim, *The Alienation of Modern Man* (New York: Monthly Review Press, 1968), 94.

The crucial point here is Dewey's honest belief that alienation is largely a psychological condition, and that the worker can once more become one with himself if the larger social significance of his labor can be shown to him. Indeed, this solution is Dewey's model throughout the essay. But alienation, as I shall show later, is not simply a psychological condition; instead, I believe alienation must be seen from a Marxist perspective as a function of production relationships. The decision to treat Dewey's essay as a cultural myth turns on his "false" understanding of alienation. Thus, it is the problem of alienation, together with Dewey's paradigm of "the new education," which establish the closed corpus for this analysis.

The next step is to provide an inventory of elements/mythemes within the narrative, so that the structure can be identified. These elements I have taken from Dewey's previously cited definition of philosophy and education. There are four elements and each fits under Dewey's rubric of educational-philosophical dispositions. Elements (1) and (2) are *intellectual* and *moral dispositions;* elements (3) and (4) are dispositions toward *nature* and *fellow man.*

Here, a parenthetical point must be made. Dewey's notion of dispositions I understand as tendencies to act which are one with the educative process. Seen in this light, the enumerated dispositions fit the previous description of elements in a cultural myth. That is, Dewey's analysis of educative dispositions are prescriptive; they tell us how the child should be formed. More than that, the narrative of the essay is didactic and therapeutic: it gives his reader an apperceptive ground. This ground is a way of viewing, making sense of, and overcoming the severe and social dislocations of an emerging industrial capitalist economy. The larger concern of specifying the mythological elements is the means for excavating the text's structure. Again, what one must look for is a set of items that share a single functional trait. These elements are never solitary, but form bundles of relations which derive their significance from their relations with each other. These elements, or "mythemes," in Levi-Strauss' terms, are the explanatory vehicles of the cultural myth. That is, cultural contradictions are explained by relating two mythemes or elements to another pair of items in a four-term homology. This homology reveals the way in which the myth is codified by exposing its binary oppositions. The transformation of these oppositions expresses the underlying thematic structure of the myth.

Reading the myth involves an understanding of the rules of combination and substitution, i.e., relations that are paradigmatic or syntagmatic. The syntagmatic reading is linear or horizontal: in the sentence, "John is a man," there is a logical order of signs. Similarly, one gets the flow of the narrative and works from a beginning toward a middle and end. Instead of the combinatory relations of syntagmatic reading, the paradigmatic relations between signs are relations of substitution and are read *vertically*. Other names could be substituted in place of John; e.g., James, Nicholas, Dominic, etc. The next structuralist move is to show how descriptions under each of the "mytheme" headings are related oppositionally and to establish a calculus of combinations. In Dewey's essay, these oppositions are transformed into a higher synthesis by a dialectic that contrasts the "old" against the "new" education. That is, the narrative descriptions are placed into appropriate vertical columns whose headings name specified dispositions. These headings are read horizontally (syntagmatically) to show the sequential ordering of the text. Reading the narratives beneath the headings, i.e., vertically, reverses the paradigmatic levels of implications.

Intellectual dispositions are placed under Mytheme bundle I. This table specifies the deadened *intellectual dispositions* of the old pedagogy and their transformation in "The New Education." "Pedagogy" and "New Education" *moral dispositions* are placed under Mytheme bundle II. The third Mytheme bundle describes *dispositions toward nature*.

Mytheme IV, *Dispositions Toward Fellow Man,* relates the contradictions between each of the old and new dispositions into a higher synthesis. Here, Dewey's psychologistic response to the problem of alienation is complete. In Dewey's problematic, the radical social change ushered in by industrial capitalism demands a radical educational change. The school must be a stabilizing order in this period of social turmoil; the school must become the embryonic democracy. In practice, this means the school children recapitulate the history of the race by learning and being trained in the adult occupations. Spared the mean economic competition of the adult world, the school nonetheless equips the children for the "physical realities of life." Now without question, Dewey understood the consequences of alienation, as Marx did. Dewey implicitly and Marx explicitly both defined alienation as the separation of self from work, separation of self from others, and separation of self from self. But from a Marxist perspective, Dewey's "problem" in "The School and Social Progress" derives from his use of categories, which mystify rather than disclose the real social relations of the culture. Dewey, here, does not allow that social relations are in the last instance production relations. Consequently, Dewey's categories function as mythic signifiers, which repress the possibility of social change because these categories psychologize alienation. Specifically, his *Dispositions*

24

Toward Fellow Man category inadequately reflects capitalist economy. Under the "fellow man" category he enumerates "old pedagogy" interests toward the individual as against the "new education" interests of the social. And Dewey hints at a class division. But again, because Dewey's instrumentalist myth does not give emphasis to the political significance of production relationships, he conflates these production relationships with apolitical *Dispositions Toward Fellow Man.*

Mytheme I	Intellectual Dispositions
Old Pedagogy	Serialized and narrow Intellectual/symbolic Subject matter/information Theory Priesthood of learning/cultured class Verbal/memory lessons
New Education	Doing, creating Producing Growth Active occupations Household model of interdependent cooperation

SOURCE: John Dewey, "The School and Social Progress," *The Child and the Curriculum and the School and Society,* Chicago: University of Chicago Press 1965.

Mytheme II	Moral Disposition
Old Pedagogy	Schooling allows one to eke out life. Moral-training emphasizes the symbolic. School is set apart from larger society. The child learns discipline.
New Education	Schooling builds character traits of industry, responsibility, and discipline from doing. Occupations are stimulated and children learn self-direction. A lovely society is built.

SOURCE: Ibid., 10.

Mytheme III	Dispositions Toward Nature
Old Pedagogy	Textbook rendering of geography.
New Education	Understanding of occupations comes through first-hand manipulation of materials found in the environment.
SOURCE: Ibid., 8.	

In order to make my own critique specific, I shall place *dispositions toward fellow man* and *production relationships* into separate tables. Mytheme bundle IV, *Dispositions Toward Fellow Man,* follows the structure of Dewey's cultural myth; it resolves alienation and marks the happy result of moving from individual estrangement to social democracy. My own Mytheme, bundle V, *Production Relationship,* is teased out of Dewey's *Dispositions Toward Fellow Men.*

Mytheme IV	Dispositions Toward Fellow Man
Old Pedagogy	Absorption in self. Passive recipiency, competition. Penalty for helping others.
New Education	Mutual help. Free communication. Outgoing energy. Education corresponds to general march-of-events. Democracy.
SOURCE: Ibid.,16.	

Dewey's search for the cause of alienation is similarly taken up by the Marxist Georg Lukács, in his, "Reification and the Consciousness of the Proletariat." Lukács, like Dewey, used the dialectic as a philosophical tool to explain change, especially to expose the subject/object relationship. For both Dewey and Lukács, the knower and the known are both moments of society and these relationships are a chiasm, a crossover or two-way relationship. Therefore, I shall synopsize and contrast specific themes within the Lukács' essay against "The School and Social Progress." This comparison allows us to reconstruct the play of mythic signifiers within the pragmatist's essay and to isolate the critical differences of specific Deweyan constructs.

Lukács' central theme is that the twentieth century alienation of modern industrial society stems from the rationalization and mechanization of production relationships. But Marx's concept of "commodity fetishism" is the core structure within Lukács' essay. In outline form, Marx's description of commodity fetishism describes the metaphysical change of the product into the commodity with a concomitant metaphysical change in the social form of labor. Under commodity form, products appear as magical fetishes because commodities are unable to derive their own value as well as the value of humans themselves. The fetishized labor product derives its value independent of both the human expenditure of production time and product quality.

Mytheme V	Production Relationships
Old Pedagogy	Cooperation is lacking. Social spirit is absent. The worker produced by this educational system is alienated; he appears to himself as an appendage to the machine.
New Education	The revolution in politics and business morality is accommodated by recapitulation of occupations. The children resuscitate the household manufacturing process: shearing sheep, carding, spinning wool. Sewing is taught to prepare homemakers. The playground shows the "natural hierarchy" of leaders and followers.
SOURCE: Ibid., 11.	

As fetishized commodity, the value of a labor product derives its comparison to a third relationship—other commodities. This value equation is determined by the comparison of any object to the commodity of commodities—money. Thus, a profound change in the social form of labor is accomplished. A product's "use value," i.e., satisfaction of immediate personal needs, is now invested with the "exchange-value" of the commodity. "Exchange-value" fluctuates according to the vagaries of "supply and demand." And the same "use-object" as a fetishized commodity becomes the autonomous entity, which defines the social relationship between humans and their labor as a social relationship between things. The crucial point is that the human being is transmogrified into a commodity whose human capacities are congested and quantified into wage labor. All commodities, including the human, are reified into "exchange-value." All commodities, including the human, become equivalent to a certain amount of money. Human labor power reified into the commodity form concretize human alienation. Specifically:

> Labor can function as a commodity only when man's manual skills, his intellectual abilities and creative capacities, in a word, the human, and qualities on which work is based, become detached from his person. They must be treated in the same way as capital, as a fund which through good management and investment will yield value.[9]

Lukács' placement of commodity fetishism into the twentieth century context ironically makes substantive connections to Dewey. As if using Dewey's own words, Lukács' is concerned about "the objective form of things and people in society . . . their relation to nature and possible relation of men to each other."[10] By reading Lukács, one immediately gets hold of Dewey's fundamental misunderstanding of alienation. Lukács sees the social relations of men and women to each other and to nature mediated by a technological commodity form. But because Dewey did not have and would not use the commodity category, other missing critical categories stunt his analysis. Most crucial is his slurring of the distinction between "use-value" and "exchange-value." Consequently, Dewey did not penetrate beneath the "rationality" of the factory system. Ironically, Dewey did not hold onto his conclusion that the worker had become a fragmented bundle of reflex operations separated from any hint at personal authorship in work. Indeed, Dewey did not recognize his own arguments as signifiers in a cultural myth, which psychologizes alienation and thereby perpetuates it.

Dewey's self-mystification on the score of "exchange-value" is ironically bound up with his plan to revolutionize education and implement social reform. He says:

> Back of the factory system lies the household and neighborhood system. Those of us who are hereby today need go back one, two or at most three generations to find a time when the household was practically the center in which were

---

[9]   Georg Lukács. *History and Class Consciousness,* trans. Rodney Livingstone (Cambridge: The MIT Press, 1976), p. 88.

[10] Dewey. "The School and Social Progress," p. 9.

carried on, or about which were clustered, all the typical forms of industrial occupations.[11]

Admitting that society has changed, he nonetheless wants the adult occupations recapitulated in the school as "active occupations of an embryonic community." He argues that, "In the school, the typical occupations followed are freed from all economic stress. The aim is not the economic value of the product, but the development of social power and insight."[12]

Lukács, on the other hand, says that fundamental social relationships are changed with the advent of technological manufacturing. That is, in the household system the economic mystification of commodities was excluded because production was geared to "use value," where "immediate personal requirements predominate."

But the educational practice of recapitulating household system occupations so that children might "develop social power and insight" glosses over the real commodity form of society. Dewey's myth represents the impossible dream. His desire for social revolution is repressed by his own categories. In its place the *recapitulation* of the old household system becomes the metaphoric signifier for a qualitatively new social order. The *similarity* between the household system and revolutionary action is in the shared community activity, the rejection of "exchange-value," and the determination of product value by humans, not commodities. As in the dream, Dewey's myth allows him to have it both ways at once. On the one hand, the desire for social revolution is fulfilled by the metaphoric signifier of recapitulation of the household system. On the other hand, the repressed significance of "exchange value" in the factory system allows Dewey to believe in the reality of a renewed community, which overcomes alienation.

Manual training is the other major signifier working within "The School and Social Progress." *Manual training* is the metonymic equivalent of rationalization of work. Dewey describes manual training of the new education as "shopwork, and the household arts—sewing and cooking." Besides engaging the children in active work, manual training prepares them for their "future vocations."[13] The end of all this is what Dewey calls "social cooperation, and constructive work attached to the ordinary conditions and motives of life." Throughout each of his examples of manual training, the children worked together on a common

---

[11]   Ibid., 18.
[12]   Ibid., 13.
[13]   Ibid., 21.

project. In Dewey's words, the children "[reinvented] the first frame for carding wool . . . redevised the simplest process for spinning the wool."[14]

The historical and experimental introduction to industry impresses on the child not only the necessity of invention, but also its effects "on the modes of social life." The result is that the child perceives the world as a place "in which everyone has a calling and occupation, something to do. Some are managers and others are subordinates."[15] The manual training signifier hides the latent metonymic signification of the rationalization of the work process itself. That is, Dewey's use of the outdated "household" model hides the fragmentation of the worker. Lukács points out that the production "use-value" can be separated in space and time. With the modern mechanical fragmentation of the work process into discrete rationally calculable operations, so too the worker becomes fragmented. The worker becomes less active and more subservient: the worker is, in Lukács words, "a mechanical part incorporated into a mechanical system." The worker finds it already pre-existing and self-sufficient; it functions independently and he or she has to conform to its laws whether they like it or not. In fact, the more precise the rational calculation of the work process, the more human qualities of the worker appear "as mere sources of error."[16]

Dewey's essay, on the other hand, resolves alienation by psychologizing it. Ruefully, Dewey laments,

> How many of the employed are today mere appendages to the machine which they operate! [He goes on] . . . it is certainly due in large part to the fact that the worker has had no opportunity to develop his imagination and sympathetic insights as to the social and scientific values found in his work.

Ironically, in this passage Dewey points out the heart of the hidden problematic within the essay. For, as I have argued above, "The School and Social Progress" does not show that he was an apologist for American capitalism, but that his text was a dream whose significance was not realized. Critical here was Dewey's joining together the mythemes of *disposition toward fellow man* with the household system of production into a new ethic. Together these elements worked as latent ideological signifiers, which mystified both Dewey and his readers' comprehension that politics are grounded first in labor, and that an increasingly rationalized and mechanized workplace mediated human

---

[14]   Ibid., 23.
[15]   Lukács, *History and Class Consciousness*, 89.
[16]   Dewey, "The School and Social Progress," 24.

production relationships through exchange-value. The consequence was that Dewey' text, like a dream, fulfilled a wish and left the world as it was.

Chapter Three continues the structuralist critique by applying Althusser's Marxist model to expose the political ideology of Afrocentricity.

Chapter 3
Althusser: Reading the Afrocentric Myth

Historically, the American educational system has reflected the racism of the larger culture. And for many Afro-American critics, not even the Supreme Court ruling of *Brown et al v. Board of Education of Topeka* (1954), which desegregated the public school system, has produced a lasting remedy. Indeed, some critics argue that the American public schools are permanently racist; specifically, they claim that the entirety of the public school socialization process privileges a white ethnocentrism and devalues the Afro-American child's experience.

One remedy has been Afrocentricity.[1] The "subject of the Afrocentric paradigm is its placement of Africa at the center of any analysis of African history and culture, including the African-American experience."[2] Proponents describe Afrocentricity as "a humanistic

---

[1]   From the various models of Afrocentricity, Molefi K. Asante's paradigm was chosen for several reasons: his work is comprehensive, widely disseminated, and easily read by a lay public.

[2]   Bayo Oyebade, "African Studies and the Afrocentric Paradigm, A Critique," *Journal of Black Studies,* 21, 2 (December 1990): 223.

philosophy, a scholarly methodology, and a model of practical action."[3]

In this chapter, I critique Molefi Kete Asante's text, *Afrocentricity*, as a curriculum model that powerfully captures the notion of education as political, social, and self-formative. Applying Louis Althusser's Marxist/structuralist technique of reading, the text is revealed as an ideological discourse meant to construct the reader's subjectivity.

My reading unpacks the ideological content of *Afrocentricity* at three levels. At the first level the text is entered again, using Levi-Strauss' construct of cultural myth. Level two exposes Althusser's connection to Lacan, emphasizing the Marxist's assimilation of the Lacanian *Imaginary*. Discussion of the *Imaginary* reveals the construction of the ego, the resolution of the Oedipus complex, and the positioning of gendered subjects in the phallocentric symbolic order of language and culture. Level three describes the work of *Afrocentricity* texts within the political context of the school as a part of the Ideological State Apparatus.

Remembering Levi-Strauss' definition of cultural myth as a ground for understanding cultural contradictions, the conditions for the reception of the Afrocentric myth are obvious: *Afrocentricity* speaks directly to black America, because it appears as the fulfillment of truths hidden. The reasons? *Afrocentricity* reveals the story of an oppressed people whose history has been fabricated, and whose language has been devalued and derived from an alien culture—many of who are today suffering the severe economic exploitation of a capitalist/racist society. Indeed, in these conditions of alienation, the young underschooled, underemployed, black youth must see the mythic ideology of the American Dream as the Great Lie; in its place *Afrocentricity* creates an ideology of hope, telling the reader who she/he is, what she/he can know, what she/he must do, and what true history is from an African perspective.

Once again, my critique of Asante's Afrocentric ideology is fundamentally political. The intent is to find answers to two questions. First, how does the Afrocentric myth work educationally as a mechanism of social and self-formation? Second, how does the practice of this ideology affect the Afrocentrist politically in the production relationships of work?

Answers to these questions begin with a look at the Afrocentric myth as an ideology or a story that one lives. Such a story is like a religion; i.e., it answers the Kantian questions "What can I know?", "What must I

---

[3]   Abu Shardow Abarry, "Afrocentricity Introduction," Ibid., 200.

do?", and "What can I hope for?" And like a religion, the myth joins one to fellow believers. This group membership is a connection that works to reinforce one's assent to the didactic, moral, and therapeutic messages about the world and one's place in it, which the myth delivers. To call Afrocentricity a religion is not hyperbole. Asante himself says "Afrocentricity can stand its ground among any ideology or religion: Marxism, Islam, Christianity, Buddhism, or Judaism. Your Afrocentricity will emerge in the presence of these other ideologies because it is from you. It is a truth even though it may not be their truth."[4] With these introductory remarks I shall begin to excavate the structure of the Afrocentric religious ideology.

The forward to the *Afrocentricity* text begins with the following moral injunction:

> The need for an Afrocentric philosophy is so great that it is impossible for me not to insist on every black person reading this book. (Why?) Afrocentricity resembles the black man, speaks to him, wants for him, what he wants for himself. Dr. Asante's book on Afrocentricity is the next step in a victorious consciousness. It is an answer to the intellectual black man who wants to know why and analyze, it is the answer to the pragmatic black who wants to know where is the ritual and the support system and whose god will I be worshipping. It gives the answer to the man and woman . . . that we must quickly return to our centers for peace in our families.[5]

Later, I will show how the religious mythic structure of *Afrocentricity* employs a pantheon of prophets, a revisionist view of historiography, a metaphysics, and an ethical system. At this point I want only to preview the ways Asante confers on Afrocentricity the status of religion by introducing the political function of a sacred text.

Asante says, Afrocentricity is the one true religion of Africans worldwide, and *Nija*—The Way—is its sacred text. Asante's arguments for these claims take this line: "[All] religions represent the deification of someone's nationalism." Language is the vehicle of national cohesion and identity. The language of Afro-Americans is Eubonics (black English) for Yoruba, for Asante the language would be Twi.[6] But Christianity speaks to believers in the European tongues and Muslim believers must speak an Arabic tongue. Both religions are contradictions

---

4   Molefi Kete Asante, *Afrocentricity* (Trenton: Africa World Press, Inc., 1988).
5   Ibid., VIII.
6   Ibid., 4.

of the lived experience of the Afrocentrist. Asante argues that *Nija,* the sacred text of Afrocentricity and that text alone, speaks to the diaspora of African peoples because it "recounts the collective experience of the world view grounded in the experience of African people"; *Nija* "represents the collective memory of the continent"; and *Nija* represents a religious commitment to the Afrocentric world view.[7] This religious structure in Afrocentricity gives believers not only a sense of community, it also appears to give them some political control over their lives. I shall argue that this is really an imaginary, ideological definition of the world. I shall introduce the examples of the Imaginary, and the famous *fort-da* game. The game analysis underscores the fullness of language in the construction of male subjectivity. I turn now to Lacan.

Chapter Two introduced Lacan's use of metonomy and metaphor in his exploration of dreams. Because it is central to Althusser's critique of ideology, what follows is a description of a prominent feature in Lacan's linguistic psychoanalytic model, namely, the Imaginary. Immediately following this, to set the stage for the feminist issues raised in Chapter Eight is Lacan's revisionist reading of Freud on the latter's description of his grandson's *fort/da* game. Here, the game will be highlighted; what emerges from this analysis is a divided subject caught in language and subject to the Symbolic order. Of necessity, what follows is a schematized version of the Imaginary; my point is to outline the *form* of Althusser's argument on the relationship between ideology and the formation of the subject. For Lacan, the formation of the subject has three movements: the pre-Oedipal or Imaginary phase, the Oedipal or Symbolic phase, and the resolution of both movements in the discourse of the unconscious.[8] Lacan begins by paying special attention to what he calls "the Mirror phase" of the Imaginary. The "Mirror phase" describes the earliest stage of Ego formation; that is, of an eight-month-old male infant enthralled by the image of his own body, which he sees reflected in the mirror. Lacan plays on the radical unity and opposition contained within the constructs of image and imaginary, showing how both are the common path of conduct in which the Imaginary is substituted for the actual. What happens is the systematic misrepresentation of the child to himself. This is an alienation rooted in the child's false belief in his own autonomy. In this illusion, the child sees a gestalt; i.e., the image of his body standing erect and moving this way or that, in a play of reflections

---

7   Ibid., 53.
8   See Jacques Lacan, *ECRITS* (New York: W.W. Norton & Company Inc., 1977).

which he controls with purpose and without hesitation. This gestalt is a lie that the child tells himself; his erect posture and his movements depend on the adult holding him before the mirror. But this illusion of his autonomous body image is so absolute that the child's consciousness pushes aside even the physical presence of the adult. Essentially this play of the body image turns reality upside down: the child is caught up by the illusion of an autonomous double; this is the Imaginary self. To call this construction Imaginary is to recognize that self understanding is mediated by the image presented to others. Ironically, it is the others who mirror, define, and shape that image. For the child, the Imaginary and the actual become equivalents. Now, obviously this child is his own body and not his image. But this is crucial, because his body is visible to others, causing a shift in conduct to occur from "the lived body to the visible body." From the perspective of the child's consciousness, a "new content and new narcissistic function makes possible a sort of alienation. [Thus, the child believes] I am no longer what I felt myself immediately to be; I am the image of myself offered by the mirror, an ideal, fictitious, imaginary me of which the specular image is outline."[9] Later, I will show the form of this psychological process is repeated with a new content, as Althusser adapts the Imaginary to decipher the politics of the subject constructed in and by ideological practices.

To complement this description and to flesh out Lacan's analysis of the emergence of subjectivity, I now move to the *fort-da* game, important for its linguistic structure of subjectivity. The *fort-da* game previews the male child's advance toward the resolution of the *Oedipus Complex.* Freud here describes his grandson using a reel to rhythmically raise up into sight an attached object and then to lower it out of sight. Symbolically, the object stands for the child's absent mother, which he can now bring back or send away at will. Raising the object into sight is greeted with the exclamation (fort) *here*! Lowering it brings forth (da) *there*! For the child, the mother is symbolically controlled at the end of a string. In Lacanian terms, the object is a *signifier;* the *signified* is demonstrated by a presence or absence.

In Lacan's revision of the *Oedipus Conflict,* the emphasis on the scopic drive, seen above in both the Imaginary and the *fort-da* game, is repeated. Forced to renounce possession of his mother because of symbolic fear of castration by his father, the male acquiesces, accepting

---

[9] J. Lacan, "Le Stade due miroir comme formateur du-fonction due je," *Revue Francaise de Psychanalyse,* 13, no. 4 (October-December, 1949), 449–455.

36

the promised substitute satisfaction of other women available in the future. The engine in all of this is language. With the acquisition of language desire is deflected; the male child gains recognition as a subject: he participates in and ratifies the Symbolic Order of culture (what Lacan also calls the Name of the Father). The male child becomes a signifier in the social scheme. Put differently, the male child's identity takes on the symbolic status of the phallus, the center of culture. In this scheme, woman is a void; in Lacan's terms the woman does not exist. I will take up this issue later in the Irigaray and Kristeva analyses. For purposes here, Althusser does not avert to this issue. Instead, alienation and the construction of identity appear as monosexual (male) political problematics.

With this preliminary data regarding myth, religion, and the Imaginary in place, I want to turn now to Althusser's analysis of ideology and its application in the critique of the Afrocentrist model.

Althusser is a structuralist-Marxist who uncovers the material role of ideology in the exploitative structures of capitalist economy. And, in the largest sense, he uses the term "ideology" to mean a material, political, psychological apperceptive ground, which is internalized by the oppressed and delivers to them a distorted picture of the real conditions of their existence. Ideology is effective whenever those who are exploited believe either nothing can be done to change their lives, or worse, that they actually have control over their lives and their existence is not one of alienation.

To locate the ideological apparatus of the capitalist economy, Althusser begins by asking, "how does the capitalist economy sustain itself? More specifically, what conditions allow capitalism to continue? And, how does the State legitimize, generate, and continuously replace an alienated labor force?" He finds answers located in the specific relations between

The *infrastructure*, or economic base (the "unity" of the productive forces and the relations of production) and the *superstructure*, which itself contains two "levels" the politico-legal (Law and the State) and ideology (the different ideologies, religious, ethical, legal, political, etc.)[10]

My analysis focuses on the superstructure for reasons that will become

---

[10]   Louis Althusser, *Lenin and Philosophy and Other Essays*, trans. Ben Brewster (New York: Monthly Review Press, 1971), 134.

apparent. The work of the superstructure, or those institutions which Althusser identifies as the Ideological State Apparatus (ISA), is not one of physical repression. The ISA is not itself the economic base. The ISA instead is a cultural mechanism of social formation: i.e., institutions within the ISA mediate, define, and legitimize the class system.

Following this definition of the ISA, the school then is a strategic institution in the superstructure; i.e., an institution whose main task is to prepare future workers by inculcating the capitalist ethos in the young.

My analysis will offer an ironic variation on this theme. I shall argue that the Afrocentric myth, when used in the classroom as the core of the curriculum, takes on the function of the superstructure as readily as the traditional classroom alluded to above. Put differently, the child who introjects the Afrocentric myth creates a self with a politically false and distorted view of the world. Adopting Lacan's work, Althusser calls this ideological deception the Imaginary. He means that the exploited classes live out an Imaginary relationship with the real conditions of their existence. In both the Afrocentric and the traditional school, the mechanism of the Imaginary is a belief system that works like a religion, complete with practices and rituals that form the child-subject. The linchpin in this system is what Althusser calls interpellation. More on the Imaginary and interpellation will follow later.

However, before exposing how the school operates as an ISA, a prior question must be resolved. Namely, "how does the state immediately produce the labor power needed to reproduce itself?" Althusser's answer and the key to understanding alienated labor is wages. Further, he inserts the wage/labor and power/value equation into historical context. Wages constitute:

> Wherewithal [sufficient] to pay for housing, food and clothing . . . is doubly historical in that it is not defined by the historical needs of the working class "recognized" by the capitalist class, but by the historical needs imposed by the proletarian class struggle (a double class struggle: against the lengthening of the working day and against the reduction of wages.)[11]

Obviously, the discussion of wages and labor power are central to the Marxist critique of the capitalism and the class division between the haves and the have-nots. I highlight it for two reasons. First, this crucial insight is the foundation on which Althusser builds his critique. And

---

[11]   Ibid., 131.

second, it similarly is crucial for my uses: as he embraces the wage-labor capitalist equation, so also Asante explicitly rejects the Marxist analysis. But as Asante presents the wage as an end both to be hoped for and to work for, his political critique of American culture is defanged. Asante at best can instill only black pride. The world stays as it is.

In his words, ". . . one of the most important economic rights in the coming decades will be the right to a salary, [and] we shall have to fight the contest for salaries. It is increasingly true with whites also that the security of salary is more important than the right to real estate."[12] As must be obvious, Asante rejects Marx. Indeed, Asante explicitly characterizes Marx as a Eurocentric materialist[13] whose analyses spoke about class conflict while neglecting white racism[14] and ignoring the unique history of the African peoples. Moreover, in Asante's view, Marx reduced the meaning of labor to manual labor and offered an eschatology that promised the victory of the working class.[15] Asante says, "Afrocentricity rejects these views; instead, it values the labor of thinkers, culture, and spirituality. [Sic] indeed," from Asante's perspective, "Marxism explains European history from a Eurocentric view; it does not explain African culture." (Moreover, the Afrocentric eschatology is nonmaterial), a "history of harmony, stemming from a strong sense of God-consciousness in nature and each other."[16]

These remarks are crucial for a number of reasons: not only is Marx's critique of culture (i.e. the superstructure) misunderstood, but the centrality of wages as the engine in the reproduction of labor power is turned upside down, and we have previewed the alpha and the omega of Afrocentricity in the spiritualism of what Asante calls Afro-collective consciousness. With this connection of the economic base to the superstructure in mind, I shall now turn to Althusser's description of the school's functions within the ISA, then making connections between the Afrocentric model and the ISA.

To put things in order, the first question to be answered is, "What are the school's prime ideological functions?" Remembering that the dominant ideology is usually not recognized (i.e. ideology defines the world "naturally" as the normal state of affairs or the taken for granted),

---

[12] M. Asante, *Afrocentricity*, 98.
[13] Ibid., 16.
[14] Ibid., 33.
[15] Ibid., 80.
[16] Ibid.

Althusser speaks about the school on two levels.

On the surface, the school functions to teach subject matter and to prepare students for careers. But to Althusser, the school's deep functions within the ISA are to transmit subject matter that is wrapped in the ruling ideology and to operate as a social sorting mechanism. Specifically, what is learnt are the basic subjects, language, arithmetic, natural history, the sciences, literature, or simply the ruling ideology in its pure state.[17] The ruling ideology is a hidden agenda secreted within the following disciplines: ethics, civics, and philosophy. Having inculcated these foundational studies as the core of the child's social formation, the school's most powerful intervention next occurs when the child reaches age sixteen (in the U.S.A. this social milestone is usually high school graduation). At this time, the school's sorting function is most explicit. Here, the child's history of "scholastic adaptation" determines life chances. Althusser's description is that of a socioeconomic matterhorn with increasingly more selective and prestigious positions nearer the summit. Winners and losers alike are provided with a specialized ideology "which suits the role it has to fulfill in class society."[18]

Proportionally, "a huge mass of children are ejected into production . . . another portion carries on . . . until it falls by the wayside [these are] petty bourgeois of all kinds." The portion that survives and reaches the summit are "the agents of exploitation (capitalists, managers), the agents of repression (soldiers, policemen, politicians, administrators, etc.), and the professional ideologist (priests of all sorts, most of whom are convinced 'laymen').[19] The school then reproduces the relations of the exploited to exploiters, repeating the capitalist relations of production, and inculcating within the child the ideology of the ruling class, wrapped up in an apprenticeship with a variety of know-how knowledge.

Each class has an ideology specific role: the exploited have. . . a highly developed professional, ethical, civic, national and a political consciousness; the role of the agent of exploitation (ability to give orders to the workers and to speak to them . . . that of the professional ideologist [has the] ability to treat consciousness with the respect, i.e. with contempt, blackmail demagogy they

[17] L. Althusser, *Lenin and Philosophy and Other Essays*, 135.
[18] Ibid., 155.
[19] Ibid.

deserve, adapted to the accents of Morality, of Virtue, of Transcendence, of the Nation . . . etc.).[20]

Of course, for most students and teachers, none of this is obvious because the school is presented as ideology free; i.e., the school is the place where teachers respect the "conscience" and freedom of those entrusted to them. Repeating the traditional school's work as an ISA, the Afrocentric model depicts power in society according to a three-term hierarchical division of intelligence. Asante says, "three types of intelligence exist in the world: Creative intelligence, Recreative intelligence, and Consumer intelligence."[21] These distinctions essentially specify the roles of those individuals, whose work is either to create, promulgate, or receive the Afrocentric ideology. Creative intelligence is the most valuable type of intelligence in that it develops one's ability to communicate with the whole earth by remaining open to associations' ideas, spaces, and possibilities. Creative intellects are "disciplined [by] attitudes rooted in Afrocentric images and symbols."[22] Examples include Aliijah Muhammad, Karenga, and King. Recreative intellectuals: poets, scholars, teachers, and artists have the task of propagating the vision of creative intellectuals. Examples include Malcolm X, Halisi, Baraka, Abernathy, and Jackson. But, the majority (by nature) is most suited as consumer intelligence types; these [people] neither create nor recreate ideas, but rather consume and utilize ideas.[23]

Curiously, the socioeconomic divisions implied in this structure are not mentioned; rather, these separations are leveled out in a unified, organic culture of Afrocentrism. Indeed, Afrocentrism is all embracing and sanctified for, "all intelligence is accepted as containing the God-force."[24]

To summarize the argument thus far, reconsider the question: how does the Afrocentric myth/curriculum work as a part of the ISA? The answers are that Afrocentrism tacitly accepts the material and political conditions of capitalism by setting down wages as the central economic reward. Afrocentrism also tacitly accepts the class structure of capitalism by promoting the divisions in society as simply manifestations of

---

[20]   Ibid., 162.
[21]   M. Asante, *Afrocentricity,* 37.
[22]   Ibid.
[23]   Ibid., 38.
[24]   Ibid.

differing kinds of intelligence, and is a quasi religion; i.e., Afrocentrism is a belief system whose practitioners are sanctified by the Afrocentric God-force. But, Afrocentricity as a religion works toward a spiritual end that does not change the believer's sociomaterial conditions. Indeed, the change that appears in the believer's material existence is, I will show, an Imaginary change.

To this point I have asserted that Afrocentricity is a myth with a message delivered as a religion. The most important evidence cited described the *Nija* as Afrocentrism's sacred text. But as I earlier suggested, my use of the term "religion" also includes a pantheon of prophets and "saints," a revision of history, a metaphysics, and an ethical system. Evidence for these claims begins with a consideration of Afrocentricity's holy figures.

The sainted in the Afrocentric pantheon range from Afro-American religious and political personages to Egyptian and Nubian figures. Notable Afro-Americans here include Martin Luther King, Jr., W.E.B. Du Bois, Aliijah Muhammad, and Malcolm X. But Asante counts as most visionary Marcus Garvey, a man whose political program articulated cultural and national liberation for Afro-Americans. Spiritual models of Afrocentricity are found in the lives of Piankhy, Nzingha, Tutankhamun, and Tinubu, as well as "ancient African priests in Egypt, Yoruba priests in Nigeria, and the Macumba priestesses of Brazil."[25]

The prophets of Afrocentricity are Karenga and Asante, himself. Speaking about the deliverance of the word to himself, Asante quotes from the Nija: "This is the Way that came to Molefi in America; The Way that came to me is how it is and how it must be for the Abibi man."[26]

Asante locates the tainted history of the diasporan black people in the politicization of the concept of race and white historiography. Race is an ideological construct, a weapon with neither biological nor anthropological validity, which has been used to legitimize the white man's oppression of the black. Indeed, white historiography has incorporated a European ethnocentrism that has distorted the truth of human history and robbed the black African of a true identity. Asante's responses to this racism appeal to Diopian historiography; his intent is to revise the story of the black African in such a way that a new sense of subjectivity will be constructed within the individual that comes through

---

[25]   Ibid., 53.
[26]   Ibid., 100.

a collective Afrocentric consciousness shared by all members of the African diaspora worldwide.[27]

He claims this "universal African consciousness is an awareness of our collective history and future,[28] i.e., a consciousness of a ". . . group of people thinking in the same general direction" that resurrects the origins of civilization in the ancient Egyptians—a black people. Asante says:

> Irrespective of present locations, the roots of all African people go back to East Africa, the cradle of human history. We do not find the Hebrews or those related to them until thousands of years after the ancient Egyptians (Africans) and Nubians (Africans) had appeared.[29]

Indeed, Eurocentric history defines the origin of human Western civilizations that Africans gave the world: Ethiopia, Nubia, Egypt, and Cush, and it is from these civilizations that medicine, science, and the concept of monarchies and divine-kingships, as well as an Almighty God, have their source.[30]

Bound up with the sacred test of the *Nija,* the stories of the prophets, and the revisionist historiography, Afrocentricity is a metaphysical principle or Spirit which is unfolding. The elements of Afrocentric Spirit are a fusion of nature in the bicameral mind or God-force, historical Africa, and the present technicultural, African American.[31] Asante claims the God-force speaks to all Africans directly in their own language,[32] and is everywhere present[33] as the continuum of the spirit and matter. In this view natural things, such as trees, have essences. There is no absolute distinction between mind and matter and all things ultimately are a part of a spiritual core.[34] But, the fullness of the Spirit is yet to come with the rise of the collective Afroconsciousness.[35] This collective consciousness of the Spirit grows toward a liberation of the African diaspora, which finds itself at the center of postmodern history.[36]

---

27 Ibid., 19, 48, 51,106.
28 Ibid., 25.
29 Ibid., 7.
30 Ibid., 39.
31 Ibid., VIII.
32 Ibid., 4.
33 Ibid., 5.
34 Ibid., 81.
35 Ibid., 29.
36 Ibid., 6.

As I have already shown, Afrocentricity combines a worldview, a political program, and an eschatology aimed at producing a new Afrocentric subjectivity. The mechanism of this identity construction is a religio-ethical system that defines correct behavior. Discussion of the Afrocentric religio-ethical system is crucial because it reveals the construction of the Afrocentric subject at two levels: a) the totality or collective consciousness, i.e., Spirit, and b) the life of the individual Afrocentric believer.

Spirit is the totality because it embraces the *Nija* text and revisionist history and behaviors (*Nija* rituals, political actions, ethical imperatives) and most especially, people who collectively identify themselves as Afrocentrists.[37]

To make sense of the relationship of collective consciousness and the ethical system of Afrocentricity, things have to be put into political contexts. To that end, I shall return to Althusser's descriptions of ideology, paying special attention to the dynamics of the religious formation of the individual subject.

Althusser specifies one institutional facet of the work of ideology in the functions of the church. Specifically, the behaviors of the believer are traced to an ultimate source in ideology. The key to all of this is the connection between the believer's ideas, his practices, church rituals, and the common source of each of these elements in ideology. To flesh out the argument I will begin with the question: what are the relationships between the believer's ideas about self and religion? Put differently, what follows from the believer's belief? Althusser says that the individual thinks his ideal religious belief has a spiritual source. Further, this is a belief that she/he (apparently) freely forms. But, true belief entails specific consequences.

> The individual in question, behaves in such and such a way, adopts such and such a practical attitude. . . participates in certain regular practices which are those of the ideological apparatus on which depend the ideas which he has . . . freely chosen.[38]

Althusser's examples cite behaviors predicated on belief; i.e., the individual goes to church, "prays, confesses, does penance."[39] Thus, the

---

[37] Ibid., 31.
[38] L. Althusser, *Lenin and Philosophy and Other Essays,* 167.
[39] Ibid.

believer's belief in what (she/he thinks that she/he freely accepts), demands that she/he act accordingly. If what one believes and what one does are not identical, then she/he appears to act on other ideas that she/he has in his/her head. In religious terms, such actions are morally culpable as inconsistent, or cynical or perverse. On the other hand, the fact that the individual's living faith is embodied in precise material actions is taken seriously, means we can see a concrete expression of the Imaginary.

Althusser argues that the Imaginary here derives from the believer's false belief that his/her ideas are spiritual and that she/he is their source. In fact, these ideas stem from a material source, the institution of the church, and the believer's belief is both verified and reflected in certain practices that are inserted in church rituals, where the believer acts insofar as he is acted on by the institution. These actions/practices rebound to the individual, publicly naming him as a believer. The believer, in Lacan's terms, becomes a *specular self,* reflecting the institution.

This act of public verification, where the individual becomes the public *specular subject* of ideology, is called by Althusser interpellation.

Interpellation records the transformation of the individual into the new subjectivity of the system. The process is dialectical: the system (church/school or other ideological institution) recognizes the individual, who now gains identity as a concrete subject. Althusser compares the experience to that of hailing someone in the street. In this example, someone "calls to another: 'Hey, you there!' The individual hailed, turns around and with this physical conversion becomes a subject. Why? Because he has recognized that the hail was really addressed to him, and that it was *really him* who was hailed."[40]

The function of this interpolation is to provide the individual with a personal identity that derives from his/her relationship to the institution. The interpellated individual now is a subject; one who occupies a certain place in the world; one who obtains recognition through his practices; and one who gains subjectivity as she/he mirrors an Absolute Subject larger than himself.

For purposes of clarity, this can be set down as an equation: Individual subject = lower case "s." Absolute subject = uppercase "S." The individual interpellated becomes a subject "s" out of his material relationship to an absolute other subject "S" (God is Althusser's religion

---

[40]   Ibid., 178.

example). The new identity of the interpellated, specular subject is "s=S=s."

My last concern is to develop the implications of this analysis for the Afrocentric model.

Throughout the text, Asante has defined the totality of Afrocentrism as God, as the collective unconsciousness, the bicameral mind, or the Spirit in time. The subject who embraces Afrocentricity is at once accepting the Spirit, understanding the world through a certain apperceptive ground, obeying certain moral imperatives, and creative a new self. Following Althusser, this ideological mechanism can be treated as a relationship between Spirit/Subject (S) and the subject/interpellated individual or true Afrocentrist believer (s).

On the other hand, the true believer whose behaviors are guided by the Afrocentist ideology not only is creating a personal subjectivity, "s," she/he is also recreating the proper Afrocentrist collective unconscious, "S." But the test of Afrocentrism is whether behavior founded on correct understanding.

Now, earlier I argued that the Afrocentric ethical system concretizes answers to the questions: "What must I do?" and "What can I hope for?" Since the Afrocentric ethical system is also a political reality as well, it appears easier to sort it out if it is treated as a mechanism with an apperceptive ground and a set of ethical imperatives. The apperceptive ground of Afrocentricity embraces everything that is good and true, and everything that can be known about the self "s" and world through the medium of African culture and toward the realization of collective consciousness, "S."

Asante says:

> All political, artistic, economic and aesthetic issues are connected to the context of Afrocentric knowledge. (This includes) everything you do, all that you are (or) will become. (Anyone who is beyond the pale)—a non-Afrocentric person (is one who) operates in a manner that is negatively predictable. The person's images, symbols, lifestyles, and manners are contradictory and thereby destructive to personal and collective growth and development." (Again and again, the point to be remembered is) "there can be no effective discussion of a united front . . . until we come to terms with the collective consciousness (S)." For the believer, the imperative is clear: you are its ultimate test. You test its authenticity by incorporating it into your behavior . . . it becomes your life because everything you do, it is.[41]

---

[41]   M. Asante, *Afrocentricity,* 66.

If the test of faith is in the willingness to obey a moral imperative, then a crucial Afrocentric reality test is whether the individual is willing to dedicate his/her life to the fulfillment of Afrocentrism. This means that the true believer must constantly be on guard, examining his/her own actions and the actions of others. Asante says, "deviations [from Afrocentrism] are intentional or unintentional misapplications of symbols and images which subvert the collective unconsciousness of our people."[42]

All that anyone can do, know, or hope for must be found in Afrocentrism. This apperceptive ground puts an ideological glaze on the most mundane experiences, from watching television to flying in an airplane. Even temporal experience is affected, i.e., if someone were to ask, "What time is it?" The complete answer must be placed in an Afrocentric context. Is the question about the ordinary time of day? i.e., "It's eight o'clock?" Or, is the question about the fulfillment of Afrocentric Spirit on Earth, i.e., "nation time"?

Indeed, this is a demanding leap of faith, with an epistemology whose logic Asante says, "is based onthe ever present reality of ourselves . . . deviations (from this faith) lead to the fog which surrounds those who wander from their centers."[43]

Such a logic is, Asante claims, immutable, non-contradictory, and consolidating. I have argued it is all of these qualities because it is a logic founded on the egocentric predicament of the Imaginary. Put differently, Afrocentrism attempts to set down the limits and conditions of what the true believer can know about the world with Afrocentrism at its center.

Thus, the Afrocentrist who truly believes creates a new individual, subjectivity, "s." This new "s" comes into being subjected to and circumscribed by the Afrocentric collective consciousness, "S." At the same time, "s" sustains "S" through this change of identity. In sum, this acceptance of Afrocentricity reflects a political commitment, a moral direction, and a new statement about psychological health. Each of the above cohere in the identity of the new Afrocentric subject = "S" + "s." But with all of these changes, the material-political existence of Afro-Americans who are without privilege remains unchanged.

My analysis of the Afrocentric curricular model has attempted to show that Afrocentricity reinforces the Afro-American's alienation.

---

[42]   Ibid., 86.
[43]   Ibid., 87.

Evidence adduced, coupled the Afrocentric curricular model to the Ideological State Apparatus. The medium of this ideology was Afrocentricity as a religious myth. Appealing first to the Imaginary construct found in Lacan, the work of the Imaginary was found in the infant's false belief in his own autonomy. The latter was reinforced by a specular image that was a lie the child accepted. Although the content has changed, the Imaginary was seen again in the Afrocentric myth. The myth provided the believer with a new but false sense of autonomy. The Afrocentric myth was then treated as a religion having a sacred text, a history, prophets, saints, rituals, an ethical system, and metaphysics. Each of these elements were seen as operative in creating the Afrocentric subject. Afrocentrism appears to improve the lot of the true believer, i.e., a new identity is forged, pride in oneself is restored, and a better understanding of the world is developed. But once again, my conclusion is that these conditions are politically Imaginary. Afrocentrism is an economic system that embraces wage-value and of consequence class divisions. Afrocentrism is an a-critical ideology, which describes the sociologic economic relationships of the new ways. The fact is that the world remains unchanged, and for most Afro-Americans without privilege, conditions of alienation are reinforced. Althusser's Marxism highlights ideology as a crucial determinant of social reality. While not rejecting the importance of production relationships, his exposition of the discourse of the mythic cultural *Imaginary* displays the critical potentials of the structuralist model.

Chapter Four recasts the definition of cultural myth, applying Roland Barthes' analysis of the two-sided, denotative and connotative structure of cultural myth. What emerges is a critique of the so-called "natural" appearance of the mechanisms of social/self formation.

Chapter 4
Barthes: Reading the Mann, Cubberley, and Deweyan Myths

This chapter uses Roland Barthes' construct of *cultural myth* to critique two important ideologies that have influenced both American pedagogical policy and practice. The first critique examines the ideology of "equal educational opportunity," as found in the primary source texts of Horace Mann and Ellwood Cubberley against "the American Dream." The second critique uncovers the mythic content of Dewey's pedagogy of history.

"Equal Opportunity for All" is the historical promise of the American public school. Tied to the *American Creed* of hard work and talent as the poor child's ticket to upward mobility, this message continues to have a ready audience and dies hard. But the reality is that the public school has historically worked to reproduce social class divisions. To make the case, I use Roland Barthes' structuralist model of critique. My intent is to expose the mythic content of seminal historical primary sources on equal opportunity written by Horace Mann and

Ellwood Cubberley against a current assessment by Walter C. Parker.

Working as a structuralist, Barthes extends Saussure's linguistic paradigm in two ways. First, he adopts the description of language as a sign system in order to read cultural phenomena. Using the triadic signifier (artifact), signified (meaning), sign (cultural significance) model, his aim is to take "gestures, musical sounds, objects and the complex associations of all these which form the content of ritual, convention or public entertainment" as languages.[1]

Second, the significations he exposes reveal a process of the political formation of the citizen, hidden between the broken connections between sign systems. Put simply, Barthes' concern is to reveal the latent mythological content overlaid on everyday life. Myth, in Barthes' use, is a form of ideology. In the broadest sense, ideology is used to mean a false understanding of socioeconomic realities, a collective illusion that works "invisibly" to legitimize the political position of the bourgeoisie. Indeed, Barthes argues that myth is an anonymous definition of the world meant to ratify capitalism as the natural order of things. Myth proclaims that the bourgeois culture is everyone's; that there are no antagonistic class interests. He argues that this ideology is all pervasive, appearing in

> our press, our films, our theater, our pulp fiction, our rituals, our justice, our remarks about the weather . . . the garments we wear—everything in everyday life. [But the crucial point is that] myth is a representation, a set of norms, which the bourgeoisie *has and makes us have* of the relations between man and the world.[2]

Practiced as a part of daily life that is taken for granted, the bourgeois myth *appears* apolitical and ahistorical. Quite simply, the bourgeois myth appears as *natural.*[3] Indeed, mythic representations induce the illusion of membership in a single class so that victims might identify with the bourgeois picture of the world. Barthes argues "it is from the moment when a typist earning twenty pounds a month *recognizes herself* in the big wedding of the bourgeoisie [that myth] achieves its full effect."[4] The upshot is that the reality of culture is changed into a picture of culture and history is changed into nature. And this image has a

---

[1] Roland Barthes, *Mythologies,* trans. Annette Lavers (New York: the Noonday Press, 1989.
[2] Ibid.
[3] Ibid.
[4] Ibid., 141.

remarkable feature: it is upside down. The status of the bourgeoisie is particular, historical; but man as represented by it is universal, eternal. Myth then is depoliticized speech, in that it gives things a natural and eternal justification, which is not that of explanation but that of a statement of fact.[5]

To decipher ideology, Barthes' technique first uses a limiting principle to establish a corpus. This means he explicitly describes material that has been gathered from one point of view only, to the exclusion of all others. His *Elements of Semiology* provides the putative example of trying to uncover the significations of French food. To establish a corpus, one makes a choice from menus in magazines, restaurants, or menus learned at home. Barthes' corpus is a specific interpretation (*parole*) constituted from the totality of polysemic possibilities (*langue*). The corpus I constituted is chosen from historical documents that have altered the course of American education. Also crucial is Barthes' use of the term "natural." Barthes uses the word in an epistemic sense, not as an ontological descriptor. That is, "natural" has a stipulative meaning: a *natural signified* is an expression of metalanguage, an ideological representation of experience. This is a specifically bourgeois definition of the world; this is a politicized picture of the world that appears as normal natural, and as always having been the case. The upshot is that the political *status quo* is a given: "it goes with saying," it is *natural*. With this introduction I shall move to an application of Barthes' method.

Barthes' essay, "The Great Family of Man," is a paradigm case of the semiology of myth.[6] The "object" deciphered is an exhibition of photographs shown in Paris, on loan from the United States. The aim of the show is to depict "the universality of human experience in the daily life of all the countries of the world. The message is that birth, death, work, knowledge, play, all are fundamental to the human condition; there is a family of man."[7] Although the images display an infinite variety, (diversity in skins, skulls, and customs are repeated to the point of an underlying exoticism), the leveling factor is that all men and women display the same archetypal behaviors the world over; there is an identical human essence shared by all. The unity of the human species moralized and sentimentalized by this exhibition tells the viewer that

---

5   Ibid., 154.
6   Ibid.
7   Ibid.

Nature, not History, is the ultimate fact of the human condition. What makes all of this mythic? Obviously, the photographs are of real people; i.e., "historical alienation; differences which are injustices."[8] As counter-examples to the myth, Barthes asks if *skin color* makes no difference, why not ask the parents of the slain civil rights worker, Emmet Till, what *they* think of the Family of Man?[9] Or if the conditions of work are universal, why not consult the North American colonials of the *Goutte d'* or district what *they* think of the Family of Man?

Barthes' explication of cultural myth depends on exposing how objects (such as the Family of Man) or practices become signs that are produced by the junction of two semiological chains. The first chain is denotation; the second is connotation. The double signification of cultural myth is produced as the first system is joined to the second system. This means that the sign of the first chain is laterally "bumped" into a new position as signifier in the second sign chain. The diagram of the Family of Man myth looks like this:

	1) SIGNIFIER	2) SIGNIFIED
Language Denotation	Photos of diverse human morphologies: skin, customs, etc.	Despite diversity, the archetypal behaviors depicted of birth, work, and death are universal to the human essence.
Myth Connotation	3) SIGN The family of Man is the fundamental reality. I) SIGNIFIER	Nature replaces history. II) SIGNIFIED
	Social/economic divisions are not real. The capitalist economy is natural. III) SIGN	

Mythically, everyone works, all share the same essence, nature replaces history, class divisions disappear, and this is the best of all possible worlds. Keeping Barthes' notion of myth in mind, I want to shift my

---

8   Ibid., 101–102.
9   Emmet Till was a fourteen-year-old Afro-American child whose 1955 abduction and horrific murder by two whites in the state of Mississippi (and the subsequent acquittal by an all-white jury of the murderers) helped launch the American civil rights movement.

analysis of primary American education texts. Beginning with Mann, my purpose is to expose the mythic structure and content of the American equal opportunity message. Horace Mann's nineteenth century crusade for the American Common School used a rhetoric that speaks to us even today, especially on the score of equal opportunity. To flesh out how his words have taken on a mythic status, I shall examine his texts: *Fifth Annual Report to the Board of Education of Massachusetts, 1842* and the *Twelfth Report to the Board of Education of Massachusetts, 1849.*

The fundamental argument of the Fifth Report asks for a statewide levy to finance the Common School of the state of Massachusetts. Mann's scheme joins communal prosperity and individual upward mobility to an educated populace. Indeed, Mann argues that not to provide equal opportunity to all the children of Massachusetts is to condemn the state itself to a secondary economic status. Put simply, the American Common School is to train the laboring classes to meet the needs of a burgeoning industrial economy. Curiously however, his tone is mixed: the rhetoric is at once nonpolitically-political. In overtly political terms, he ties the American Common School to a legacy of the democratic ethos; yet, simultaneously, the capitalist economy is presented nonpolitically as a natural condition of life.

The political rhetoric reads: "The inequality in the means of education possessed by the children in the different towns and sections of the state is a subject of great moment? [Why? Because the founding fathers argued that] political advantages should be equal, and then, that celebrity or obscurity, wealth or poverty should depend on individual merit. [However], the most influential and decisive measure for equalizing the original opportunities of men, . . . is equality in the means of education."[10] But the problem that Mann confronted was that poorer and more sparsely populated districts could not support the school without government assistance. And even worse, other districts simply failed to comply with the law by employing unapproved teachers, "diverting school moneys to illegal purposes and resisting a uniformity of books."[11] Secreted here almost as an afterthought is the onus placed on the individual. "If equal opportunities of improvement are offered to all, the responsibility of using or neglecting them may just be cast on

---

[10]   Horace Mann, "Twelfth Annual Report to the Board of Education of Massachusetts," in *Justice Ideology and Education,* ed. Edward Stevens and George H. Wood (New York: McGraw-Hill, Inc. 1995), 137.

[11]   Ibid.

each individual."[12] The theme of individual responsibility continues to be hard today and it seems now, as then, to be apolitical. I will return to this later. But the core of Mann's argument, which can be reduced to a slogan repeated throughout the *Nation at Risk Report, 1983*, is clear: the schools must provide an educated workforce for the nation to prosper. The ideological stuff of this rhetoric derives from Mann's marriage of the Calvinist ethos to the needs of the emerging capitalist industrial state: a spiritually correct life demands work. And, whether one is among the elect (which is not merited) is signaled by one's prosperity. At this point, Mann ties the school to business interests. His acceptance of a natural hierarchy of capitalist over laborer is crucial; moreover, he prescribes an explicit model for the commodification of the worker in which individual human value is equated with profit for the employer. He says, "the capitalist[s] are looking for the greatest amount of labor or the largest amount of money from their investments [the worker]; they do not promote a dunce to a station where he will destroy raw material or slacken industry."[13]

By contrast, "those [workers] with a good common school education rise to a higher and higher point."[14] The American Dream, then, is the natural conclusion of capitalism and its attendant features of the profit motive, class division, and the commodification of human life—all of which are tied to the public school.

However, it is too simplistic to brand Mann as a vulgar apologist for the capitalist state. His vision penetrated into a capitalist system of *haves* and *have nots,* and the middle-class divisions accepted so naturally in the Fifth Report are precisely what he attacks about European economies in the Twelfth Report. The bottom line in the Twelfth Report is a plea for the "physical well-being" of all the people of Massachusetts. Here, Mann argues for a morally correct capitalism he calls the Massachusetts Theory, which he contrasts against the evils of Europe. The report is a warning: American capitalists are imitating their European counterparts and the democracy is at risk. Under the European theory, some are rich and many are wanting. Mann characterizes this as un-Christian and

---

[12] Ibid.
[13] Ibid., 28.
[14] Ibid.

54

heathen.[15] The riches of the European state take precedence over the population. The decadence of Europe is revealed in its

> splendid treasures and golden regalia [in England], the Tower of London and
> Windsor Palace, [in France] the Louvre and Versailles . . . while thousands [in
> these countries and the rest of Europe] . . . are dying of starvation. [Mann
> attributes this condition to the European theory] . . . in which men are divided
> into classes, some to toil and earn, others to seize and enjoy.[16]

This evil, Mann argues, is being reproduced in the United States as American capitalists emulate Europe. "The manufacturer farmer prescribes the rate of wages he will give his work people, [and] he reduces those wages under whatever pretext he pleases. [The consequence is that a social chasm exists in which one class possesses] all the wealth and education and the other become servile dependents."[17] Resentment then grows between the propertied and the laboring classes. But Mann's Massachusetts Theory is meant to provide universal education with riches for all as the counterweight to class antagonism. The myth diagrammed:

Language Denotation	1. SIGNIFIER European theory is built on class division and is an immoral economy.	2. SIGNIFIED America is emulating Europe in its division of have/have nots.
Myth Connotation	3. SIGN Massachusetts theory of reform needed for just society. I. SIGNIFIER	Universal education civilizes/provides equal opportunity for all. II. SIGNIFIED
	Schools produce riches and a morally correct capitalism. III. SIGN	

To summarize, equal opportunity in Mann presents antagonistic moral

---

[15] Horace Mann, "Twelfth Annual Report to the Board of Education of Massachusetts," in *Justice Ideology and Education,* ed. Edward Stevens and George H. Wood (New York: McGraw-Hill, Inc., 1995), 137.
[16] Ibid., 139.
[17] Ibid.

imperatives. The overarching value is the capitalist ethos. The state is the instrument of education and the common school is the highway to prosperity for all. Ultimately, whether one succeeds or not, is the individual's responsibility; the inherent contradiction in Mann's utopian capitalism is an economy that does not produce class divisions.

This problematic view takes an opposite twist in Ellwood Cubberley's scheme for the governance of the American school. His 1916 article, "The Organization of School Boards," ensconces a business model for the operation of the schools that turns equal opportunity on its head, while claiming the opposite.

Cubberley wants a reform in the method of selecting those who serve on school boards. His stated intent is to *depoliticize* school board operations and to make them more efficient and representative of the community. But a closer look shows Cubberley's plan is both political in its motivation and antiegalitarian in its implementation. Cubberley's first reform is to reduce the size of school boards. He argues, "a small board of [5 to 7 men] is in every way more effective and more efficient body than a large one."[18] His reasons: within a large body "real thinking ... planning ... executing is usually done by one half-dozen to half score of men."[19] Such a group is less talkative, will not shift responsibility for its actions to others, will not apportion out patronage, *and will not become "a public debating society."* Coupled with the smaller board, Cubberley wants an at-large system of representation to replace the ward system that is in its place. But, his argument is a special pleading class analysis of power distribution. That analysis polarizes the city into two groups: the saved and the damned. The saved are the businessmen; successful and temperate, they want strong government. Such men represent the best characteristics of the population and are motivated to act for the good of the whole city. Such men want an at-large system, but would not serve on a ward-elected board whose "management of a school system is political, or personal or petty."[20]

Living apart from the best, the damned are the laboring classes characterized as an unsuccessful and intemperate lot. Cubberley describes their wards as "the fighting third," "the red fourth," "socialist,"

---

[18] Ellwood Cubberley, "The Organization of School Boards," in *Justice, Ideology and Education*, ed. Edward Stevens and George H. Wood (New York: McGraw-Hill, Inc. 1995), 225.

[19] Ibid.

[20] Ibid., 228.

and "the high-brow fifth." This shorthand characterology describes the anarchical temper of such men who promote strife, represent only their ward, and who are constantly directed toward securing funds, teachers, and janitors for the schools they represent.[21] To clinch the argument, Cubberley includes a demographic map of the city's wards. The prominent feature is of railway tracks that separate the upper two-thirds of the city from the lower. "Negro ward shacks," "saloons and tenements," and the "red-light district" represent the damned living on the wrong side of the tracks.

Cubberley's argument has all of the elements of political myth previously stated: nature, human essence, a morally correct capitalism, and a depoliticized culture. To legitimate his argument, he employs a bourgeois reality principle that shows his version of events deriving from experience, i.e., nature. Malefactors and enlightened men actualize potentialities that are simply their human essence. The enlightened businessmen decide how the schools are to be run. And in a move that effectively *disenfranchises* the malefactors or *laboring class,* Cubberley describes his scheme as one that *removes politics from education.*

	1) SIGNIFIER	2) SIGNIFIED
Language Denotation	Ward electoral system is corrupt.	Schools are governed by inefficient political factions, including bad elements.
Myth Connotation	3) SIGN An apolitical at-large system is needed. I. SIGNIFIER	Elected businessmen working bi-partisanly know what is best for all school constituencies. II. SIGNIFIED
	A morally correct capitalism is sustained by equal opportunity schools. III. SIGN	

Today, arguments advanced by Mann and Cubberley appear too baldly undemocratic to even the most unsophisticated. For example, an embryonic scheme implied in Mann's paradigm is the track system of student placement and curricula. But, this device has been unmasked as a

---

[21] Ibid., 227.

de facto mechanism of political repression imposed on poor and minority students; i.e., those in the lowest tracks (overwhelming minorities) receive an inferior education, which prevents access to middle-class status.

Now, seemingly more democratic schemes meant to better serve the poor minority students are in place. The latter is the subject of Walter C. Parker's essay, "The Urban Curriculum and the Allocation Functioning of Schools, 1985."[22] Ironically, his analysis of the urban curriculum fits my description as a postmodern version on the American mythic theme of equal educational opportunity. Parker's essay summarizes the equal opportunity mythology reduced to the following political terms:

> Democracy asks individuals to act as if social mobility were universally possible; status is to be won by individual effort, and rewards are to accrue to those who try. But democratic societies also need selective training institutions and hierarchical work organizations permit increasingly fewer persons to succeed at ascending levels. Situations of opportunity are also situations of denial and failure.[23]

As his example, Parker cites a so-called "effective" inner-city school, George Washington Carver High School of Atlanta, Georgia. Populated by inner city minorities and poor, the school has received "attention from Congress, the press and scholars."[24] But, Parker questions if such a school is really effective. Certainly the school presents a specially designed curriculum tailored to the needs of these students, but he asks if this is a sufficient knowledge base for entrance into the middle-class. Parker claims programs such as Carver's may mask the school's real political function, which is that of managing the contradiction between aspiration and denial.

His demonstration hinges on a comparison of the school's function to a con game. The con game includes the following players: a victim (called a con or a mark), the con artist or perpetrator, and the con artist's confederate (the cooler). Once the con realizes something is wrong, i.e., that she/he has been victimized by a fraudulent game, the cooler steps in.

---

[22] Walter C. Parker, "The Urban Curriculum and the Allocating Functions of Schools," in *Justice, Ideology and Education*, ed. Edward Stevens and George H. Wood (New York: McGraw-Hill, Inc. 1995).
[23] Ibid., 179.
[24] Ibid., 180.

The cooler's job it to befriend the mark, to keep him from calling the authorities or in some other way blowing the whistle on the con game.[25]

The analogy to the specialized inner-city curriculum is obvious. Parker reads this curriculum as inadequate; in his view, these students are prevented from acquiring legitimate knowledge, i.e., the kind that provides a foundation for entrance into a baccalaureate program as well as future middle-class status/employment. The paradigm case is that of the junior college minority student. On completing the coursework, she/he is denied entry into a four-year college, leaving the individual to appear as the one who failed. In fact, the inadequacies of the specialized inner-city curricula come back to haunt the victim who is told and believes that she/he is inadequate. "Those who are denied their aspirations [are] skillfully handled so as to mollify them and adapt them to failure while the structural inevitability of their failure is concealed from them."[26] Counselors act as coolers, who reduce the student mark's sense of failure by providing alternatives, counseling, and consolation. Their task is to let the less successful "be made to feel that their failure to attain was a personal failure. This reduces their inclination to inveigh against the system that first raised aspirations, only to shut the door."[27]

Thus, the school promotes the availability of the American Dream, while channeling vertical mobility within society.

	1) SIGNIFIER Schools provide aspiration/knowledge	2) SIGNIFIED Minority/poor need special curricula to equalize chances
Language		
Myth	3) SIGN American Dream is available to all. I) SIGNIFIER	Spaces are limited to the best. II) SIGNIFIED
	Failure of the poor/minority student is individualized not institutional. III) SIGN	

This analysis can be encapsulated by quoting Paulo Freire:

---

[25]   Ibid., 181.
[26]   Ibid., 179.
[27]   Ibid.

> There is no such thing as a neutral education process. Education either functions as an instrument which is used to facilitate the integration of the younger generation into the logic of the present system and being about conformity to it, or it becomes . . . a means to [transform] their world.[28]

Indeed, in this final variation the equal opportunity myth is an instrument of conformity to the present system: the school performs its sorting function and essentializes the poor/minority student as not ready to move up, validates bourgeois political hegemony, reproduces class division, and presents this representation of the world as natural and apolitical.

Using two seminal primary texts and a topical example, I have attempted to demythologize the idea of equal educational opportunity. I applied Barthes' critical model first to Horace Mann, then to Ellwood Cubberley, and finally to Walter C. Parker's work. Mann's work espouses the common school as the vehicle to protect both a capitalist industrial economy and individual upward mobility. Cubberley argues for a new way of governing the schools that would impose a business model, simultaneously disenfranchising poor and minorities, while claiming to make opportunity more readily available. Parker reveals the connection between the fiction of equal opportunity and the sorting function of the school. And, despite historical variations of emphasis, the Equal Education Opportunity myth retains certain commonalities.

It is a bitter irony that the legacy of equal educational opportunity remains a myth. On the other hand, the origins of that myth lie in the desire for a democratic society, long ingrained in the American collective unconsciousness. John Dewey's imprint on this ethos can be seen even today.

The next section examines Dewey on the teaching of history and its relation to democracy from Barthes' critical perspective.

Dewey describes democracy as "that way of life by which experience is studied while it is also enlarged [and] enriched and to which all contribute." He meant his words both as an "end-in view" and as an ethical idea that each succeeding generation must take up as it attempts to overcome the distinctions of class, race, and economic division. Accordingly, Dewey argued that the schools must build scientific habits of problem solving and moral character in youth. To the question, "What kinds of subject matter promote democracy?" one of his

---

[28]   Ibid.

consistent answers is the *scientific study and application of history*. But although he wrote much about a *scientific* account of history, his advice to teachers regarding the *teaching of history* is skimpy. Indeed, his thoughts on this subject are most complete in the single, brief, and neglected piece, "History for Educators."[29] But so important is this condensation of his views on the subject, that it reappears as the dominant theme in seven of the chapters of his masterwork, *Democracy and Education*.

	1) SIGNIFIER	2) SIGNIFIED
Language Denotation	Capitalist economy of socioeconomic classes is natural.	Education provides the vehicle for cultural riches.
Myth Connotation	3) SIGN Educational opportunity is available to all, regardless of sex, race, and class. I) SIGNIFIER	The culture is a meriocratic system. Success or failure is the result of individual talent, work, intelligence, and drive. II) SIGNIFIED
	The poor/minorities who do not advance are individually blameworthy: they receive both the education and social position they deserve. III) SIGN	

Dewey used the essay to translate his genetic theory of historiography into specific teaching methods. Emblematic of the rest of Dewey's work, his message now is taken for granted, yet something meant to articulate for real. In a word, the essay has become a cultural artifact—which works as a myth. Taken seriously, the pedagogical application of Dewey's essay today turns his intentions upside down:

---

[29] John Dewey, *Democracy and Education* (New York: MacMillan Co; 1938), p. 378. Pedagogy is treated explicitly in "The Nature of Method," pp.168–179 and "The Nature of Subject Matter," pp.180–193. The relationship between schooling and work is found in "Play and Work in the Curriculum," pp.194–206 and "Vocational Aspects of Education," pp.306–320. The subject matter of history is dealt with in "The Significance of Geography and History," pp.207–208 and "Physical and Social Studies: Naturalism and Humanism," pp.277–290.

social critique becomes an apologia for the status-quo. To make sense of these claims I shall apply Barthes' technique of reading Dewey's text *History for Educators* as a cultural myth.

To reinforce the connection between history and cultural myth, I have chosen the example of a famous photograph that appeared on the cover of the popular French magazine, *Paris Match*. The image is of a young black man in some distant outpost wearing the uniform of the French army, his eyes fixed on the *tri-colore*. The literal meaning of the first sign is produced as the reader's perceptual act transforms certain colors and shapes into a pictorial image. The first sign's message is:

> A black soldier is saluting. [But Barthes says the connoted meaning of the second sign is:] I see very well what [this photograph] signified to me: that France is a great empire, that all her sons, without any color discrimination, serve faithfully under her flag, and that there is no better answer to the detractors of an alleged colonialism than the zeal this young black shows in serving his so-called oppressors.[30]

Like all cultural myths, the message presented to the reader appears at once as both an alibi and something natural. The alibi is that the purpose of the cover is not ideological: the photograph is really quite ordinary. One simply has to look at the magazine cover as a recording of an everyday natural event: "This is merely the image of a black man serving somewhere in the French empire." But Barthes sees through this lie, comparing it to the alibi of the "innocent" who claims she only wears a fur coat to keep warm. What really comes through in the second semiological system of the *Paris March* covers is Frenchness itself, intermixed with raw jingoism.

Barthes is careful to point out that this double system of myth represents not a suppression of meaning but a

> constant hide-and-seek between the meaning and the form which defines the myth, [moreover] the form of the myth is not a symbol. That is to say, the soldier's image is too spontaneous, too innocent, too real, too much given in the flesh. [But] . . . at a distance . . . it recedes a little, it becomes the accomplice of a concept which it comes to fully armed, French imperiality: once made use of, it becomes artificial.[31]

---

[30]   Roland Barthes, *Mythologies*, trans. A. Lavers (New York: Hill and Wang, 1973), 116.

[31]   Ibid., 118.

In this magazine cover example, history is not defined, instead a stock image is used to banalize history by giving it a simplistic narrative form. The natural order of things is reinstated. The daily evidences of class divisions are erased by images and messages such as that of the black soldier. Ironically, Barthes says that myth in a bourgeois society is depoliticized speech. He means that mythic speech turns things upside down. The *pseudo-physis* social world constructed by myth

> circulates as the antithesis of a political language, that antithesis is itself
> political, especially so when a strategy of inversion uses systems of denotation
> to fabricate the illusion of a depoliticized utterance.[32]

Keeping Barthes' notion of myth in mind, I want to shift to a description of Dewey's views on history, looking particularly at connections to democracy, ethics, and the genetic method. My purpose is to expose the limits and conditions that framed Dewey's discussion of teaching in "History for Educators."

Dewey honestly believed in the ongoing "moral progress of man," which could only be captured in a past-future continuum. Not surprisingly, then, he argued that the historian must tell a linear, sequential story—a factual account ordered by a "fundamental conception that controls the determination of a subject matter."[33] Dewey also believed that the temporal movement of history is dialectical:

> The past is of logical necessity the past-of-the present, and the present is the
> past-of-a-future-living present. The idea of the continuity of history entails this
> conclusion necessarily. [And] the present state of affairs is in some respect the
> *present* limit-to-which; but it is itself a moving limit. As historical, it is
> becoming something which a future historian may take as a limit *ab quo* in a
> temporal continuum.[34]

While the historian can only write about the past from within her/his own present, "History would most naturally become of ethical value in teaching" as it "exposes the entire advance of humanity from savagery to civilization."[35] In other words, the discipline of history is to be used as

---

32   Steven Ungar, *Roland Barthes: The Professor of Desire* (Lincoln and London: University of Nebraska Press, 1983), 27.

33   John Dewey, *Logic: The Theory of Inquiry* (New York: Henry Holt and Co., 1938), 234.

34   Ibid.

35   John Dewey, *Democracy and Education* (New York: The Free Press, 1916), 254.

an instrument that not only sheds light on ethical problems, but also moves the culture toward the realization of democracy.

Democracy is Dewey's naturalistic *Geist:* the practical and historical unfolding of what it means to be a human; that is, democracy is Dewey's metaphysic, a principle which actualizes "forces inherent in human nature." And democracy is a moral entity—a measure of "institutions as they exist and of plans of betterment."[36] Moreover, the criticisms of the moral ideal of democracy "are in fact criticisms of the imperfect realization it has so far achieved." As a consequence, Dewey argues that the practical task of democracy is one with the imperative to preserve the continuity of experience itself: democracy must be "readapted and restated in terms of present day life."

In this context, history has a double meaning:

> History is that which happened in the past and it is the intellectual reconstruction of these happenings at a subsequent time. [But] the notion that historical inquiry simply restates the events that once happened as they actually happen is incredibly naïve.[37]

The reason: the historian's selection of materials and reconstruction of the past becomes itself part of what happens historically. Put differently, historical explanation lays down specific directions with regard to the ethical significance of the past-present-future continuum. If democracy is the end-in-view, then the historian must project the direction of movement toward the future by exposing the progressive realization of this ideal in the past. Toward this end, Dewey advocates the genetic method. Again, his purpose is to show the ethical significance of history. He does this by guaranteeing the scientific necessity of the genetic account. Then he explains the application of the genetic method to human conduct. Dewey's identification of the genetic method with science is built on the themes of prediction and control and the historical evolution of human values as responses to specific conditions. He defines the genetic account as that method which "is concerned with the manner or process by which anything comes into experienced existence."[38]

---

36   Ibid., 100.

37   Dewey, *Logic,* 236.

38   John Dewey, "The Evolutionary Method as Applied to Morality," *The Philosophical Review* 11, no. 2 (1902): 109.

The object of the method is at once scientific, practical, and ethical. Its purpose

> is primarily to give intellectual control—the ability to interpret phenomena and secondarily, practical control—that is, the ability to secure desirable and avoid undesirable future consequences. [In the physical sciences, this is accomplished by experimentation] . . .taking an unanalyzed total fact [and showing] the exact and exclusive conditions of its origin.[39]

The meaning of the "thing" derives from its relation to a larger historical continuum. Moreover, the predictive value of the scientific method is one with instrumental efficiency in the interpretation of other facts that operate under similar conditions. But the physical scientist cannot directly inspect, dissect, or recombine spiritual values. Dewey says, "they are, therefore, outside the scope of science *except* so far as amenable to historic method."[40] Thus, the genetic method details the movement of ethical practices in their historical development. Like physical experimentation, the specification of the "earlier terms of the series, answers the purpose of synthetic recombination under increasingly complex conditions."[41] Out of this control, an insight into the operations and conditions that make for morality is provided. Such a control is practiced insofar as it specifies the means to modify individual and social conduct by moving that conduct toward ethically desirable directions.

The practical application of the genetic method to human conduct is placed in proper context by asking Dewey certain questions. First, what constitutes a moral judgment? Second, what is the source of the moral idea? Third, what function does history play here? Dewey answers that those moral judgments

> are judgments of ways to act, of things to do, of habits to form, or ends to cultivate. Whatever modifies the judgment, the conviction, the interpretation, the criticism, modifies conduct. To control our judgments of conduct, our estimates of habit, deed, and purpose is in so far forth to direct conduct itself.[42]

But, both individually and collectively, moral judgments represent

---

[39] Ibid., 123.
[40] Ibid.
[41] Ibid., 124.
[42] Ibid., 371.

the adjustments humans make to the demands imposed by specific historical situations. These judgments express "an attitude of moral consciousness: which is embodied in practices, beliefs, and rituals." Moreover, this moral consciousness

> maintains and reinforces certain conditions and modifies others. It becomes a stimulus which provokes new modes of action—now we see why and how the belief came about and also knew what else came about because of it. We have a hold on the worth of the belief. [43]

The genetic method applied to history allows us to grasp the past circumstances that generated a moral idea. And the method itself becomes an instrument for weighing present and future moral beliefs and judgments. The essence of the process, like the direction of human history itself, is continuous with the need to preserve the continuity of experience. For Dewey, this means the evolutionary as well as the present practical application of the moral idea of democracy itself.

But does Dewey successfully translate the moral idea of democracy into the teaching of history? To answer this question I shall now turn to his piece "History for Educators." To begin, both the aim and methods of teaching history must be specified. Dewey answers that the aim of historical instruction is to enable the child to:

(A) appreciate the values of social life,
(B) see the forces that favor men's effective cooperation with one another, and
(C) understand the sorts of character that help and hold back.

In sum, history is taught to give the child a genetic account that will lay bare the processes that produced the present cultural scene, emphasizing how the economic and industrial aspects of history expose democracy.

But remember, Dewey is preoccupied with the problem of making the cultural past connect to the child's present and future. The emphasis on the continuous relationship of past values, customs, and institutions with the present is his key premise. What Dewey wants transmitted to the young by the study of history is not simply the knowledge and customs of the group; he also wants a moral imperative transmitted so that the child develops the habits of thinking, feeling, and acting that derive from

---

[43]   Dewey, "History for the Educator," 2.

the lived conjoint experience and practice of democracy. But Dewey knew that the problem of understanding history is especially difficult for the child. Indeed, he says that for the child, nothing is as vivid and demanding as the present. Further, Dewey says teaching history as a record of the past makes no dent on the present; it only reinforces the experience of the past as dead and gone. When presented as rote, the material of history fails to promote democratic interaction.

To overcome these difficulties, Dewey's pedagogy first dramatizes industrial history, then moves to a specialized use of biography and literature, and ends with a chronological account of history geared to the child's cognitive growth. My explication will focus on the significations of the first two techniques.

The dramatic technique uses the child's natural interest in role-playing and has him/her actively re-present the cultural story. What is learned is not only how the race historically has defined needs and ends and developed instruments to obtain those ends, but also how the transformed human environment presents new demands for adjustment. Most significantly, however, the child re-presents "the ethical record" of the culture.

The complete unpacking of democracy with the stress on the historic and moral transformation of the individual and collective experience is the key to Dewey's dramatic technique. The dramatic technique is a form of play-acting that uses the child's interest "in the way in which men lived, the new inventions they made, [and] the transformation of life that arose from the power and leisure thus gained."[44] Dewey believed that the child's dramatization of historical processes, including the use of ready-at-hand materials, would open up the social world by showing "how much it cost, [and] how much effort and thought lie back of it." To do this, Dewey turns to the natural environment. Nature is the ready-at-hand equipment that the child is to manipulate in order to re-present the historical unfolding of the culture. Historical understanding is expressed by the child's own action that repeats "the point of view (of) those who lived in the past" by re-enacting the activities and production.[45] The child remakes utensils, rehandles materials, and reproduces manufacturing processes. In this activity, "he understands [those who went before and] their problems and their successes only by seeing what

---

[44]   Ibid.
[45]   Ibid.

obstacles and what resources they had from nature."[46] That is, Dewey has the children re-create the conditions of the historical past; through a specialized play-acting, including the use of real tools in natural settings, the children together repeat the creation and use of both labor relationships and inventions developed in an earlier time. Through the repetition of "the cultural play," the child grasps the motivations of previous performers in the cultural story of democracy and the child participates in a plot that is still unfolding.

But the real crux is that these activities, as Dewey presents them, hang together as an elaborate morality play that the children act out. The child is at once in two separate but interconnected worlds. On the one hand, the child is living in the present with all of its pressing demands. But, in playing, the child never completely loses sight of the fact that the role itself is "make believe." On the other hand, to re-create properly the role of another who lived in the historical past, the child must comprehend the historical other's motives. These motives make the past real in the child's imagination, yielding "a vivid picture of how and why men did this and so, achieved their successes and came to their failures."[47] The child translates motives as character models in a double sense. Motives serve not only as vehicles of "plot" development in the historical text; motives also appear as ethical ideas that the child can emulate. In fact, Dewey wants the child to see in motives "typical relations, conditions and activities," again the democratic character.[48]

The second technique is the reading of biography. Biography "as a dramatic summary of social needs and achievements pictures the social defects and problems that clamored for the man and the ways in which the individual met the emergency." But what must be avoided, Dewey emphasizes, is "any tendency to swamp history in myth, fairy story, and merely literary renderings."[49] He warns, if the aim of historical instruction is a factual account of how "those who worked in the past [are] close to those beings with whom [the child] is daily associated and [to confer] on him the gift of sympathetic penetration [of his lived experience]" then the stress on lives of individual Superheroes who are separated from the social environment inverts that purpose.[50] The proper

[46] Ibid.
[47] Ibid., 1.
[48] Ibid., 3.
[49] Ibid., 2.
[50] Ibid.

use of biography demonstrates to the child how a certain historical subject universalizes what typical people thought, felt, and did.

Dewey next considers the uses of literature in the teaching of history. He argues that literature has only peripheral value and should be used only to put "the finishing touches on factual materials. His argument juxtaposes the irreconcilable epistemic claims of narrative literature against narrative history. And Dewey is convinced by the obvious. The obvious is that the narrative claims of history are verified or falsified by reference to the facts. But literary claims are without the appeal to facts and must be verified by the sense of the fictional account. Consequently, Dewey very nearly rejects the use of fiction, saving it only for "background use" in the elementary history curriculum.

Ironically, Dewey attempts to show *Robinson Crusoe* and "Hiawatha" as prime examples of the literary disease of swamping the social aim of history "in myth." All that he will allow is that *Crusoe* represents the archetype of the American colonial, a

man who has achieved civilization . . . but [who] is suddenly thrown back on his own resources; having to cope with a raw and often hostile nature, and to regain success by sheer intelligence, energy, and persistence of character. [Moreover, he reduces the value of "Hiawatha" to only] . . . the beauty of a purely literary presentation.[His conclusion is obvious: the factual historical story] . . . must stand out on its own account.[Because history is the real, it has a] . . . more vivid and lasting value for life. Literature can only give history idealized and culminating touches.[51]

Certainly Dewey's concern is not with giving children a scientific paradigm for the study of history. What he wants to do is to explicate the unnoticed practices of everyday life. These practices are not analytical schemes in our heads. Instead, they are noncognitive, shared belief systems, i.e., social usages that answer the question "What does it mean to be human in this culture?"

At bottom, history taught at the elementary level is a form of indoctrination. Dewey certainly knew that, and said as much: "the aim of historical instruction is to enable the child to appreciate [and internalize] the values of social life." What Dewey could not know is that his techniques of teaching history are actually cultural myths.

This becomes clearer if first the transcendental ground of Dewey's historical pedagogy is specified and then translated into semiological

---

[51]   Ibid., 3.

systems. Both Dewey's dramatic and biographical techniques aim at developing in the child an understanding of his/her oneness with others. Specifically, Dewey's sense of what it means to be part of the culture originates with the social relationships embodied in production. To get hold of this, the child must be made to see history as a dynamic story of how men and women together transform nature and produce a human world through work: "when history is conceived as dynamic, as moving, its economic and industrial aspects are emphasized."[52] Like Marx, Dewey predicates culture on the human's sensuous, practical activity, or *praxis* (production). For both Dewey and Marx, production is necessitated by the human's metabolism with nature; and they both argue that one's participation with others in the process of transforming the natural world alters one's consciousness. In Dewey's dramatic technique, the children embody themselves in work and they grasp the value of the product or service directly. Because the activity is concrete, communal, and historically connected, the children also see production relations regulated directly. This unmediated relationship of self to work, self to other, and self to self is the ethical goal Dewey equates with the practice of democracy within the classroom.

In fact, Dewey's historical pedagogy recapitulates the preindustrial context of the agrarian family, carding sheep, spinning wool, and making candles. In Dewey's model, the child who reads about, or simulates, a past agrarian economy actually recapitulates the interdependent social system of a putative democracy while believing it to be real in his own life. That is, the ethical reality-ideal in Dewey's curriculum is that of the unalienated social relationship of men and women to each other in the historical construction of culture. Most particularly, it is the direct or unmediated regulation of workers to their production and, therefore, to each other, which appears to the child as historical fact. In fact, this is the criterion of successful teaching: history "must be an indirect sociology— a study of society which lays bare its process of becoming *and its modes of organization.*[53]

In this light, I shall discuss the cultural myth secreted in Dewey's pedagogy by treating his techniques as semiological systems. In the dramatic technique, the literal meaning or first sign produced by the child reads: "Previous generations had to provide themselves with food, clothing, and shelter. By acting out the processes of invention and work

---

[52]   Ibid., 2.
[53]   Ibid., 1.

in the classroom, I now can see how they survived. This intelligent, interdependent way of living is democracy." The second sign or mythic message connoted in the dramatic technique is: "The interdependent nature of democracy is one with the direct (unmediated) social relationships of work, and this is the way democracy works today." In schematized form the dramatic technique reads:

1.SIGNIFIER Classroom reinvention and use of tools	2.SIGNIFIED Communal problem solving	
3.SIGN I.SIGNIFIER The interdependent process of democracy		II.SIGNIFIED Unmediated social relations of production
III.SIGN This is the way democracy works today		

In the biography technique, the literal meaning of the first sign reads: "This is a true story of a real person. His/her actions with others were intelligent and had desirable moral consequences. The culture strives toward this democratic ideal." The mythic message connoted by the second sign reads: "The culture strives toward this democratic ideal. Emulate this moral behavior. Moral behaviors, not production relationships, determine capitalist democracy."

In schematized form the biographical technique reads:

1.SIGNIFIER This is a true story of a real person	2.SIGNIFIED His/her actions were intelligent and moral	
3.SIGN I.SIGNIFIER The culture strives toward this democratic ideal		II.SIGNIFIED Emulate this moral behavior
III.SIGN Moral behaviors, not production relationships, determine capitalist democracy		

Indeed, it is such "depoliticized" "factual" biographies that carry the heaviest ideological baggage. The truths of these biographies work as proverbs that legitimate the *status quo*.

Now, I do not intend the above to mean that Dewey was an apologist for capitalism; even a cursory reading of his essays in *The Social Frontier* provides evidence of his sustained critique of capitalism. However, although Dewey, like Marx, stresses economic and material relationships, he simply lacks the categories Marx used to get at the fullness of production relationships, especially *commodity fetishism.*

In simple terms, Marx's description of commodity fetishism describes the metaphysical change of the product into the commodity with a concomitant metaphysical change in the social form of labor. Under commodity form, products appear as magical fetishes because commodities are unable to derive their own value as well as the value of humans themselves. As fetishized commodity, the value of a labor product is determined by the comparison of any object to the commodity of commodities, money. Thus, a profound change in the social form of labor is accomplished. A product's "use-value," i.e., satisfaction of immediate personal needs, is now invested with the "exchange-value" of the commodity. "Exchange-value" fluctuates according to the vagaries of "supply and demand." And the same "use-object" as a fetishized commodity becomes the autonomous entity that defines the social relationship between humans and their labor as a social relationship between things. The crucial point is that the human being is transmogrified into a commodity whose human capacities are congealed and quantified into wage labor. All commodities including the human, are reified into "exchange-value." All commodities including the human become equivalent into a certain amount of money. Human labor power reified into the commodity form concretizes human alienation.

> Labor can function as a commodity only when man's manual skills, his intellectual abilities and creative capacities in a word the human qualities on which work is based, become detached from his person. They must be treated in the same way as capital, as a fund which through good management and investment will yield value.[54]

Reading Marx, one immediately gets hold of Dewey's fundamental misunderstanding of capitalism. Marx sees the social relations of men and women to each other and to nature mediated by a commodity form. But because Dewey did not have and could not use the commodity

---

[54] See George Lukács, *History and Class Consciousness*, trans. Rodney Livingstone (Cambridge: MIT University Press, 1976), 88.

category, other fundamental mistakes stud his analysis. Dewey's criticism of industrial capitalism made no distinction between "use-value" and "exchange-value." Consequently, Dewey did not penetrate beneath the "rationality" of the factory system. And Dewey could not recognize his own pedagogical techniques as signs in a cultural myth that legitimates the class divisions of bourgeois capitalism. His self-mystification on the score of "exchange-value" is ironically bound up with his plan to implement democratic action in the classroom. Allowing that society has changed, he nonetheless wants preindustrial familial relationships recapitulated in the school as living models of democracy. In fact, in a parallel essay he says:

> In the school the typical occupations followed are freed from all economic stress. The aim is not the economic value of the products, but the development of social power and insight.[55]

Dewey, like Marx, understood that fundamental social relationships are changed with the advent of manufacturing. But, in an agrarian economy (Dewey's model) the mystification of commodities was excluded because production was geared to "use-value" in which immediate personal requirements predominate. But Dewey's historical pedagogy glosses over the real commodity form of society, and Dewey's model of democratic action is blunted by his own categories. The dramatic recapitulation of inventions and the reading of biographies are meant to signal a new social order. Certainly, the similarity between Dewey's techniques of teaching history and democracy is reflected in the shared community activities of the classroom. But Dewey's intellectual arsenal lacked the categories of "exchange-value" and "commodity fetishism." Consequently, the realization of a bourgeois capitalist morality is shown by the child's internalization of the messages produced by Dewey's dramatic and biographic techniques. For the teacher, Dewey's historical pedagogy appears as a natural and taken-for-granted part of the American intellectual landscape. In practice, his historical pedagogy becomes a cultural myth that legitimatizes the *status quo*.

My reading Barthes' cultural myth repeats the Marxist theme of the duplicity of social constructions or myths in everyday life as appearing natural. Of course, his point is that the power and political place of the

---

[55] John Dewey, "The School and Social Progress," in *The Child and the Curriculum and the School and Society* (Chicago: The University of Chicago Press, 1971), 18.

bourgeoisie is being protected and justified. And, Barthes was not a Marxist; his strategies are fundamentally semiological. Barthes' emphasis on connotation not only echoes the anti-essentialism of Jean Paul Sartre, but also previews a markedly poststructuralist theme of the instability of so-called final and ultimate meanings.

Chapter Five returns to the aesthetical dimension and the relationship between language and perception, as first discussed in the Merleau-Ponty chapter. The concern is to apply Foucault's micropolitics of critique to a different side of the school's formation of subjectivity. That is, how the institution's need to assess the child's reading readiness is tied to a discursive practice that has political consequences.

Chapter 5
Foucault:
Reading Magritte,
Reading Readiness

This chapter applies Michel Foucault's analysis of the surrealist painter René Magritte as a model of pedagogical critique. The discourse examined is the California Reading Readiness Test, which is given to kindergarten children. The intent is twofold: first, to expose the relationship between figurative and linguistic meaning; secondly, to show the critical power of Foucault's model, discovering how the implementation of this standardized test fits what Foucault calls a normalizing practice.[1] With these purposes in mind, I shall begin by contextualizing Foucault.

Michel Foucault's philosophical investigation represents a turn from structuralism to poststructuralism. He retains the structuralist emphasis on language (more specifically discourse), but his method of critique is idiosyncratic. Fundamentally, he investigates discourse to expose it as

---

[1]   The model chosen here is taken from Michel Foucault, *This is Not a Pipe,* trans. James Harkness (Los Angeles: University of California Press, 1982).

the medium of both political power and the source of the creation of the subject. But to get hold of what he is doing, it is important to set down what he has rejected. The Marxist category of production, the Kantian schema of the Transcendental Subject, the formal binarism of structuralism, and even the humanist model of the free subject are all left behind.

Foucault is more properly a historian of the history of ideas. His influences include positivist historiography, psychoanalysis, phenomenology, surrealism, and structuralism. Further, his investigations of insanity and sexuality are landmarks in late twentieth century thought.

Foucault characterizes his work as archeological and genealogical. The archeological method excavates the historical conditions that make possible a given discourse. The genealogical method, on the other hand, exposes dominant theories that create, discipline, and subjugate the individual. Again, central is his concern about the relation of language to the sources of political power.

Themes treated below present both a difference and a linkage with the issues previously raised: perception, aesthetics, and language. Together, these ideas create an aesthetics of critical pedagogy.

In broad terms, this notion of an aesthetics of critical pedagogy is rooted in the experience of contradiction, which one experiences before certain works of art. This contradictory experience has an active/passive dynamism.[2] One actively forms perceptions and simultaneously one undergoes a new, changed way of experiencing. The trigger of this critical experience is the art object itself: the painting, play, film, book, or dance presents contradictory meanings.[3] The consequence is that one's habitual, unreflective ways of viewing the world are changed. The model of this experience can be used to form a critical consciousness with new understandings of work, self, and others. For example, Magritte's paintings often confuse and provoke because he destroys ingrained notions about art, representation, and logic.

Art is popularly conceived as the human activity of imposing order on experience. Moreover, the aesthetic experience is defined as essentially contemplative: Wordsworth's definition of poetry as "emotion recollected in tranquility" is a powerful statement that is still

---

[2]   See John Dewey, *Art as Experience* (New York: G.P. Putnam's Sons, 1958).
[3]   See Robert Hughes, *The Shock of the New* (New York: Alfred A. Knopf, Inc., 1991), 16.

accepted today.[4]

In this vein, representation is the aim of the artist. Representation as well is the standard of excellence. That is, the novel or painting is "made well" if it appears to successfully repeat, copy, or imitate an original thing—something real in the world. Doubtless, this view comes to us from Aristotle's *Poetics,* where he writes that "poetry, tragedy, copy, are all in their general conception modes of imitation. Indeed, Aristotle describes artists as individuals who "imitate and represent various objects through the medium of colour and form, and taken as a whole imitation is produced by rhythm, language, or harmony."[5] Now, while there is no obvious linkage between logic and art, later discussion will show that Magritte integrates imagery and sentences within the same work. Indeed, the net effect of this conjunction is an exercise in contradiction. Anticipating my discussion of Magritte then, a few words on the function of logic follow.

Logic is an instrument of reason whose rules must be obeyed if we are to think correctly. That is, when we come to true conclusions it is because we have put together correct judgments about what is the case. The necessary conditions here involve the valid conjunction between the quantifier, the subject, the copula, and the predicate. Hence, the sentence "John is a man," is to be logically translated as the subject is a member of/or joined to the larger class of *men.*[6]

These allusions to contradiction made above are perhaps made stronger if we compare Magritte's paintings to lies. Magritte's paintings repeat within us the agonizing experience felt when we think the friend conversing with us is lying. This agony courses through us because we want to believe him/her, and we think we have contradictory evidence, but we are not sure, not positive. In this situation, our interlocutor's arguments may assume such a perverse plausibility that we at once accept and reject them. Similarly, looking at a Magritte, one senses a wrenching anomaly in the paradox: "If I am lying is true, it is false and false if it is true." What is demanded here is that a distinction be made between language about language and words in a speaker's concrete

---

[4] See William Wordsworth, "Michael, A Pastoral Poem," in *Dominant Types in British and American Literature*, ed. William Davenport, et al. (New York: Harper & Brothers, 1949), 109.

[5] See Aristotle, *Poetics* 1447a-1447b, in *Philosophy of Art and Aesthetics*, ed. Frank A. Tillman and Steven Cahn (New York: Harper and Row, 1969), 58–59.

[6] See Daniel J. Sullivan, *Fundamentals of Logic* (New York: McGraw-Hill, 1963).

situation. The issue concerns the relationship between words and things and truth. The philosopher's remedy of course is to appeal to the law of contradiction (P cannot be both true and false).

But Magritte has no truck with the solidity of the laws of logic. His paintings are built on contradiction. That is, within the same canvas one may find a realistic tableau of ordinary life and written below it a descriptive legend.[7] The contradiction of course comes from the title's explicit rejection of what we may believe we are seeing.

To make specific how the Magritte/Foucault aesthetics of contradiction works, I shall now turn to Foucault's description of paradigm case, his painting, "The Treachery of Images."

Ceci n'est pas une pipe.

René Magritte, "The Treachery of Images."
© 2001 C. Herscovici, Brussels/Artists Rights Society (ARS), New York.

At first glance, the pipe depicted appears so accurate, so detailed in shape, color, and volume, that it seems like a photograph tacked onto the canvas. But, beneath the pipe is a single sentence written in cursive: "This is Not a Pipe."

Indeed, this sentence is not a legend that amplifies the pictorial image. Foucault says the statement seems so simpleminded, one first wonders why it has been made: "Of course, this is an image of a pipe, not a real pipe," is the viewer's first response. But, Foucault is not satisfied. He is interested in how the contradictory *text* of the imagery and the discourse that "names" it are to be construed. His central argument is that Magritte's meticulous depiction of the "Pipe" is not

---

[7] M. Foucault, *This Is Not a Pipe,* 24.

representational. Remember, Foucault's argument derives from the contradiction of viewing the "Pipe" and reading its inscription.

If one takes the claim of the legend, "This Is Not a Pipe" seriously, three things emerge: first, "this" particular painting of a pipe does not stand for or represent any of that class of objects found in the world, that are called pipes.[8] Second, "this," the sentence itself could not, not represent a pipe.[9] Finally, "this" mixed element of discourse and image, written pipe and drawn text, "is not a pipe."[10]

What is the point? Foucault wants to show the systems of imagery and language cancel each other in Magritte's painting. *More precisely, since the Renaissance, imagery in realistic painting has implied resemblance to actual things in the world, and language discourse has been used referentially to name and affirm the contents of painting.* But, in "The Treachery of Images," resemblance and discourse are dissociated and ruptured.

Given these contradictions, how is one to view "Pipe"? What replaces resemblance or copies of things? Foucault's answer is similitude. The contrast between resemblance and similitude is illustrative. "Resemblance serves representation, which rules over it; resemblance predicates itself on a model it must return to and reveal; and resemblance presupposes a primary reference that prescribes and classes."[11]

In contradistinction, "Similitude obeys no hierarchy, it develops in a series."[12] Similitude does not take as its standard something copied, an original found in the world. In such a case, one could arrange copies hierarchically according to degree of resemblance. Specifically in the "Pipe" painting, what is crucial is that the pipe be seen as a text/simulcrum. Foucault says, "this is not a pipe"; rather, it is a text that simulates a pipe, a drawing of a pipe (drawn other than as a drawing) that is the simulcrum of a pipe (drawn after a pipe that itself would be other than a drawing).[13] *To say the pipe image is a simulacrum is to say that it belongs to the order of things that are similar, i.e., other drawings of pipes,* i.e., the order of similitude.

---

[8]   Ibid., 26.
[9]   Ibid., 27.
[10]   Ibid.
[11]   Ibid., 44.
[12]   Ibid.
[13]   Ibid., 49.

A summary of the above serves to put the Foucault/Magritte critical aesthetic in relief. The salient points are:

(1) Plastic imagery and discourse can be shown as incommensurable sign systems;

(2) Plastic imagery need not represent; it can be an expression of similitude;

(3) The deliberate juxtaposition of a plastic text against a discourse which annuls the "meaning" of that text breaks down previously held beliefs about the function of painting. Further, this demolition of resemblance . . ."the affirming and representing nothing," is a critical moment in the viewer's consciousness.[14] I use the term *critical* to mean a question about the limits and conditions of what can be known.

Until now, I have dealt only with the mechanical core of the Foucault/Magritte aesthetic. Returning to the main concern of this chapter, i.e., a critical pedagogy, I shall argue that the teacher who possesses this critical aesthetic consciousness develops a new understanding of the hidden power relationships embedded in the imagery and language of the California Achievement Test Form 10.[15]

McGraw-Hill's Examiner's Manual legitimates the use of this CAT, appealing to the instrument's validity, its match with curricular content, and its usefulness in designing coursework to meet the needs of students. Because these claims represent data to be integrated into the Foucaultian critique, their evidence is listed below.[16]

---

[14] *California Achievement Tests,* Form E., Level 10, Examiner's Manual (Monterey, California: CTB/McGraw-Hill, 1985), 1.

[15] *California Achievement Tests,* Form E., Level 10, Examiner's Manual (Monterey, California: CTB/McGraw-Hill, 1985), 1.

[16] This critique is not intended to be an attempt to demonize the California Achievement Tests, Form E, Level 10. Strategies of observation, examination, and normalizing judgment in schools provide increases in student achievement. Whether or not this is domination, Foucault says varies according to each specific case. Michel Foucault, "The Ethic of Care for the Self as a Practice of Freedom: An Interview with Michel Foucault on January 20, 1984," in *The Final Foucault*, ed. James Bernauer and David Rasmussen (Cambridge: MIT Press, 1988). Discussing criticism of the pedagogical institution, Foucault says: "I don't see where evil is in the practice of someone who in a given game of truth, knowing more than another, tells him what he must do, teaches him, transmits knowledge to him, and communicates skills to him. The problem is rather to know how you are to avoid in these practices—where power cannot play and where it is not evil in itself—the

Validity of this CAT is shown in its combination of "the most useful characteristics of norm referenced and criterion referenced tests [that] provide information about the instructional needs of students."[17] Moreover, this test measures "achievement in basic skills commonly found in state and district curricula."[18] Content categories themselves are found in "current state and curricular guides, published texts, [and] instructional programs [all of which were subjected to] criterion referenced assessment instruments."[19] Most important, this test "establishes reference points for beginning instruction in kindergarten, [and this can be used] to predict first grade reading achievement."[20]

Form E, Level 10 is divided into six sections. Five of these sections assess the child's language skills as indicators of reading readiness.[21] All of the language elements tested are rooted in Standard English. The critique will be trained on the section called "language expression." This choice is made because each of the other sections (sound/visual recognition. Vocabulary, and comprehension) coalesce in the child's lived experience of expression.

The teacher's manual describes the language expression section as one that measures "a student's understanding of singular and plural nouns, and past, present and future verb tenses. [This is done] as the student identifies the picture that is associated with correct usage."[22] *Put differently, the child's choice is one that attempts to match a correct verbal description with a picture representation.* Directions are read aloud to the child by an examiner who asks the child to mark a correct selection. The following are sample instructions and pictorial representations meant to assess the child's understanding of verbal tense. Keeping the following item chart in mind, consider how the test items must appear to a kindergarten inner-city Afro-American child. Quite simply, the language expression section does not make sense. Why? Fundamentally, the Standard English of the test is not the language that he/she uses. This child's native tongue is black English/Eubonics.

---

effects of domination that will make a child subject to the arbitrary and useless authority of a teacher. Ibid., p. 18.

[17] *California Achievement Tests*, Form E, Level 10, Examination Manual (Monterey, California).

[18] Ibid.

[19] Ibid.

[20] Ibid.

[21] Ibid., p. 2.

[22] Ibid.

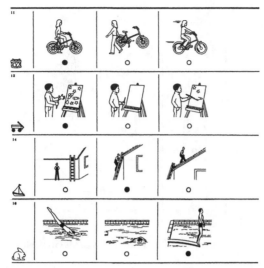

California Achievement Test, Form E. CTB/McGraw/Hill.

An analysis of the syntactic differences between Black English/Eubonics and Standard American English demonstrates striking disparities, especially in the origins and structure of verbs. One expert, J.L. Dillard, says, "Black English reveals the greatest difference from white American dialects—and the closest resemblance to its pidgin and Creole answers in its system of verbs."[23] Particularly significant here are the usages that render tense.

The CAT examples, as cited, render the present as "the man *is* climbing" and "the boat *is* sinking." But, in Black English, the sentence would read: "the man *be* climbing" and "the boat *be* sinking." Another example of the present tense, "John *runs*," as expressed in Standard American English, would be "John *run*," in Black English. Not only is the sentence structure different, notice the "*s*" ending is dropped. But, the test earlier treated the "*s*" ending *only* as a measure of the child's ability to distinguish singular and plural.[24]

[23] J.L. Dillard, "Black English" review of *Black English* by Toni Cade Bambara, *The New York Times*, 3 September 1972, p. 3.
[24] *California Achievement Tests*, 2.

82

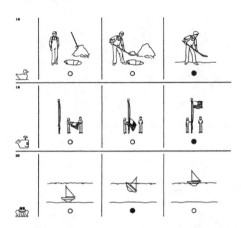

California Achievement Test, Form E. CTB/McGraw/Hill.

One finds similar disparities when comparing the future tense and the idiosyncratic Black English use of "done." The CAT example, as previously cited, rendered the future as: "the girl *will* ride" and "the man *will* dive." In Black English, these same sentences would read: "the girl *be* riding later" or "the man *be* diving later." A similar disparity is reflected in the handling of the past tense. The Standard English version, "I *have* gone," in Black English becomes "I *done* gone." Setting the Black English usage against the CAT items: "the boy painted" and "the children raised," makes explicit linguistically different structures; "done" is not used in Standard English in this way.

As must be obvious, the kindergarten inner-city Afro-American child who depends upon the Black English code cannot make much sense of the CAT items; she/he is forced to guess the correct response in Standard English. The conclusion to be drawn is that the CAT does not adequately assess the reading readiness of this population. None of this implies that McGraw-Hill, the publisher of the CAT, failed to address concerns about test bias. In prefatory comments describing the CAT, McGraw-Hill describes its effort to reduce test bias. Specifically, it enlisted men and women representing "various ethnic groups and who held responsible positions in the educational community to identify within the test, items they considered to reflect bias in language, subject matter, or representation of people."[25] The publisher also indicates that those items

---

[25]   Ibid., p. 4.

that appeared to be biased were eliminated.[26]

My task is not to fault, blame, or accuse McGraw-Hill of producing a biased test. Such an assertion would be false and falls into the trap of a single causation explanation; this would be much like labeling McGraw-Hill the Marxist superstructure.

Item 11	The examiner is directed to say: "Move your marker down to the drum. Look at the pictures. Find the picture that shows the girl will ride the bicycle. Mark your answer."[27]
Item 12	The child is asked to match the correct illustration with the following sentence: "The boy painted a picture."[28]
Item 14	The illustration here is to be matched with the sentence: "The man is climbing a ladder."[29]
Item 16	The item sentence is: "The man will dive into the water."[30] This form continues throughout the section. The description for items 18, 19, and 20 follow.
Item 18	"The man will dig a hole."[31]
Item 19	"The child raised the flag."[32]
Item 20	"The boat is sinking."[33]

Foucault's critical apparatus is more nuanced. Moreover, the discussion of the CAT as a school practice/discourse has yet to be connected to Foucault's aesthetic of contradiction.

To bring everything together, a distinction about purpose is necessary. A stated purpose throughout has been to show how this contextualized CAT practice is an instance of normalization. But my overarching purpose is to expose the core aesthetic element within Foucault's critical apparatus, namely the ambiguous, contradictory, and nonrepresentational relationship between words and things. To set the stage for all of this, I shall first return to the CAT practice using Foucault's categories.

---

[26]   Ibid.
[27]   Ibid., 17.
[28]   Ibid., 39.
[29]   Ibid.
[30]   Ibid.
[31]   Ibid., 40.
[32]   Ibid.
[33]   Ibid.

Making sense of this contextualized activity in Foucault's terms means looking at this standardized practice as a political text. This is a text which experts design, administer, and interpret, creating a certain kind of subject. To begin, the CAT, the minority child, Black and Standard English codes, as well as the school, must be seen as parts of a system with interlocking institutions, techniques, social groups, and perceptual organizations. All of these elements are orchestrated by rules of discursive practice.

The administration of the CAT brings about an *anonymous alliance* between the institutions of the publishing house and its psychologists, who design the test, and the school's agents.[34] The latter include the examiner, who administers the test, the psychologist, who interprets the scores, and the teacher, who defines the meaning of the test by placing the child into a certain reading group. That these groups share common perceptual organizations is shown not only by the schools' continued use of this test, but also by the phenomenon of cooperating representative minority members from within the educational community who screened the test for racial bias and then gave their imprimatur.

Parts 1, 2, and 4 of the CAT Examiner's Manual give explicit descriptions of the test [Part I], preparations to be used by the examiner before administering the test [Part II], and procedures to be used to process completed tests [Part III]. These sections do more than describe, they prescribe and impose rules of discursive practice. That is, they are serious speech acts, set down by serious speakers who prescribe not only what must be said, but also what can be said and how it is to be said. Certain examples appearing in the preparation and description sections are typical. The preparation section describes a nonvalid test as follows: "A non-valid test results when a student loses time during that test or marks answers randomly. [Examiners are instructed to treat these conditions as a non-valid test result and to] erase all answer marks for the affected test section."[35]

The development section describes how test items were chosen, accepted, and scientifically validated:

---

[34]   Ibid. 3.
[35]   Ibid. 7.

All items and test directions were carefully reviewed for content and editorial accuracy. A staff of professional item writers—teachers experienced in the test's content areas—researched and wrote items.[36]

Test vocabulary was "controlled by reference to *Basic Reading Vocabularies* and *The Living Word Vocabulary*." The scientific validity of the item selection "involved the application of Item Response Theory (IRT) and the implementation of a three-parameter statistical model that takes into account item discrimination, difficulty and guessing."[37]

To call these descriptions a discursive practice is to repeat that certain truth conditions were set down by experts (serious speakers) speaking as experts about the testing of children (serious speech acts). And, finally, these speakers validate this practice as neutral scientific statements when they invoke the item response theory method.

Reading this experience, one finds the political mechanism that Foucault has named normalization. Under the rubric of science, normalization uses totalizing procedures of classification and supervision to define normality and to impose remediation. The result is the creation of a certain kind of person or subject.

Normalization is implicit in the goals of this CAT: measuring achievement in basic skills, determining reading readiness and providing information about the instructional needs of children. These expert definitions of goals and test procedures operate to create a system that defines and classifies subjects, measures abilities, and exposes those skills that are below the norm. No single instrument seems more efficient and helpful in the prediction of a child's potential for achievement, and the control of conditions to bring about optimum development so early in the child's career. The CAT is education as a normal science.

But such normalization also defines the deviant, the abnormal, and the problem, each of which falls outside of the norm. The kindergarten child whose primary code is Black English *must* fail the language section of this CAT. But the specific problem demonstrates the particular within the universal: *one minority child's deficiency represents the school's overarching problem with a competing code.* A typical solution is devaluation; i.e., Black English is the rejection of

---

[36] Ibid., 3.
[37] Ibid.

A network of cultural loyalties, group outlooks, verbal games, perceptual modes, lore, logic, structure, grammar, music—the language habitually used to perceive, record, remember, transmit, abstract, recall and relate by at least eighty percent of Black Americans.[38]

In Foucault's terms, normalization is the anonymous expression of power; it is not McGraw-Hill, the teacher administering the test, or the psychologist/teachers who interpret it. *Everyone and no one* express this power, which is the rule of silence, and censorship, a power that operates according to the mechanism of taboo. The subject created by these practices is a child with a language problem whose scores are below the norm, a child needing remediation. Remediation is efficient and scientific, in so far as it silences the child's mother tongue.

At this point, the arguments have shown how the discursive practice of the CAT has created a definition of the minority child. This is an *institutional construction of the child's subjectivity* that is held in place and articulated through such nondiscursive practices as the school's track system and the placement of the child into remediation programs.

At first glance, nothing here seems connected to the Foucault/Magritte critical aesthetic, outlined in the beginning. But, Magritte's painting, "The Treachery of Images," was meant as a paradigm case that would expose the hidden power relationships embedded in the imagery and language of the California Achievement Test Form 10. All of this is made plain by showing how the constructs in both the Foucault and Magritte texts overlap, share common origins, and are mutually implicated. Using these convergences I will show the crux of Foucault's argument on his rejection of the naïve correspondence between words and things.

The relationships I have in mind, like those between the painting and the CAT example are speech acts that overturn the logic of representation, express lies, and are most adequately seen as similitudes. Calling the CAT example a discursive formation by implication is also to call it a speech act. In uttering words (giving and taking tests, interpreting scores, and "placing the child") actions are performed. So too the painting must be seen as a speech act as the viewer reads the sentence, "This is not a Pipe." What seems a simple declarative sentence is really an imperative—an order to behave in a certain way. The viewer is told: "Do not believe this is a pipe; do not accept this faithful

---

[38]   J.L. Dillard, "Black English," 3.

representation of real pipes as other than a lie." Once again, the pictorial correspondence between the painted image and the linguistic naming of that image are sets of contradictions. This contradictory speech act is repeated in a different form by the minority child who is asked to connect the CAT imagery with appropriate words.

The lie for the child is the forced choice of words, the forced options that name the image with words she/he does not use. But if the child cannot join the CAT pictures to correct captions, then the premise on which the test was built, namely its representational power, is contradicted as well. Now, although this example of the minority child's experience is a lie, it is a weak lie. The argument assumes that if the child were competent in Standard English, she/he could match the image and sentence correctly. The implication is that representation remains intact. The stronger sense of this lie is evident in placing the "pipe" and CAT examples against the logical paradox cited originally, i.e., "I am lying is true; if it is false and false if it is true." Remember the description-imperative of the title, "This Is Not a Pipe," is meant to be taken as a true statement. The viewer's immediate response is one of doubt. What she/he sees is an apparent contradiction: This pipe image is not to be seen as representing real pipes. The logical translation: If this image is a lie is true, it is false to believe it is a representation. Foucault's conclusion, then, is that the text of the imagery and words falls apart. The significance of the Foucault critical aesthetic here is evident in contrasting effects. The ordinary move is to define the child's Black English code as substandard. This judgment is then validated by appealing to the child's poor CAT performance.

But following Foucault's "Pipe" lesson, something different happens. Here, the teacher assumes an attitude of doubt puts the meaning of the minority child's low score out of play. Further, with the teacher's acceptance of Black English as a language, the representational power of the CAT itself is questioned. With this, the cycle of normalization stops. As an aside to all of this, I am not advocating that the child avoid becoming competent in Standard English. Methods of code switching in appropriate ways is what the schools should teach the African-American children, especially those in the central city schools. But this is not what the example is about. The subject of this chapter is the kindergarten child, who by definition comes ill-equipped to switch from Black English to Standard English. This inability to switch codes is normalized as the child's lack of readiness and underachievement. But following the

"Pipe" paradigm, normalization stands revealed as a political process. Moreover, the lesson of the Foucault-Magritte critical aesthetic is not that words are joined to things in a naïve correspondence; instead, it is the understanding that the language of discursive practice creates the reality it describes. The lesson: kindergarten minority children who lack language skills may be the creation of practice whose authors are anonymous. But these nameless agents' power defines human possibilities. Foucault's critical aesthetic is a powerful tool that can be used to overcome this lie.

The appeal of Foucault's critique lies in its analysis of the micro-politics of classroom practice. That is, he shows the reader how power is insinuated within knowledge. He shows how discourse is bound up with a certain *episteme*. The latter is a transcendental ground that lays out the limits and conditions of what can be thought, what can be said, and who can say it. Foucault maps this out historically. The irony is that power is displaced from superstructure and cannot be located using an overarching *grand narrative*. For Foucault, the superstructure is no longer isolable and the origins of power are anonymous.

Chapter Six extends the previous critiques toward new conclusions in Jean Baudrillard's analysis of postindustrial life at the end of the twentieth century. Subjectivity is caught in the consumer loop of electronic cyberspace.

Chapter 6
Baudrillard: Reading the Hyper-Reality of Dewey's Pedagogy of Occupations

Democracy and Education describes John Dewey's idea of the methods the schools must use to overcome the radical social changes affected by the industrial revolution. The overarching solution is what he calls a "New Education"—a student-centered pedagogy of doing. A crucial element of this pedagogy involves a nostalgic return to the past, in which children simulate the adult occupations of an agrarian household economy as the living model of democracy.

To observe that the present information revolution brought about by the electronic media of computers and television has ushered in a *postindustrial era,* is a truism that has become a cliché. Having said that, the question I want to raise is whether Dewey's occupation simulation pedagogy still works in an American classroom, whose children are described and see themselves as consumers.[1] The key to this analysis is

---

[1]   Two pieces of anecdotal evidence from the classroom are illustrative. In the sixth grade classrooms serviced by my students, a rather overt social hierarchy is

the treatment of Dewey's occupation simulation pedagogy as a cultural sign system that can be decoded. I shall argue that this simulation pedagogy turns Dewey's social critique on its head by reinforcing the political *status quo*.

To make sense of these claims, I shall describe Jean Baudrillard's semiological paradigm, the three orders of simulacra, and apply this schema to Dewey's pedagogy of occupations found in *Democracy and Education,* and his earlier collection of essays entitled, *The Child and the Curriculum, The School and Society.*[2] But first I shall present an overview of Baudrillard's semiotic method, emphasizing his dialogue with Saussure and Marx. Following the structuralist model, he views culture as a symbolic system: customs, institutions, images, bodies, objects, everything gains sense when it becomes a sign. That is, when each or any of the above are placed into the sign relationship of *sign* and *signified.*[3] Meaning, then, is generated out of the sign equivalence. For instance, if a five-dollar bill has value, it is because that piece of green and white paper is a *signifier* made equivalent to a certain amount of labor time, *the signified.* Again, this represents not a natural value, but one that emerges out of relations of equivalence.[4]

In sum, the purpose of cultural semiology "is to make explicit the implicit knowledge used in the reading of signs. Furthermore, its task is to uncover our conceptual space."[5] In this structuralist context, Baudrillard overturns a central element in the Marxist critique, namely, the *use-value/exchange-value* distinction. Recall for Marx, *use-value* meant something found in nature and having the potential, when worked

---

observed. The children often tease and provoke each other regarding the quality of sneakers, shirts, or jackets that are worn. The provocation is signaled by the display of (or lack of) famous brand name logos. Furthermore, the New York State Department of Education describes disabled students who receive services as *consumers.*

[2] See J. Baudrillard, *Simulations* (New York: Semiotext (e) Inc., 1983).

[3] See C. Levi-Strauss "Introduction a L'oeuvre de Marcel Mauss," in *Sociologie et Anthropologie*, ed. M. Mauss. (Paris: Presses Universitaires de France, 1950), XIX.

[4] See R.D. D'Amico, *Marx and Philosophy of Culture* (Gainsville: University Presses of Florida, 1981).

[5] J. Culler "The Linguistic Basis of Structuralism," in *Structuralism: An Introduction* ed. D. Robey (London: Oxford University Press, 1972), 28.

on, to be changed into a product that satisfies human needs. Marx's example is the process whereby wood is changed into a table. *Exchange-value* signaled the change of a product into a commodity. The commodity bought and sold takes its value from another commodity: gold/money. Together with the abstract economic law of supply and demand, it ultimately determines even the value of humans themselves.

Reemphasizing the structuralist's insistence that meaning is marked by a relational system of differences within a language, Baudrillard translates Marx's *commodity form* into a *linguistic form* of symbolic exchange. Central in all of this is the notion of consumption, which is the stage where the commodity is produced as a sign, and signs (culture) are produced as commodities. Baudrillard says, contrary to Marx, that *use-value* does not exist prior to exchange value; *use-value* is insinuated within *exchange-value;* use-value props up exchange-value; it is produced as a sign. Commodities are signs that connote different hierarchical relationships between individuals. Culture itself is reducible to the production and consumption of signs. Fashion, architecture, books, and health regimes—everything falls under consumption. But the central example is cultural recycling; that is, the signs of the cultural past that are now reproduced as simulation. The Las Vegas recreation of Venice is an example. Even nature itself is not immune. Baudrillard argues that nature is no longer a primeval and original presence symbolically opposed to culture, but a simulation model, a consommé of the recirculated signs of nature. The latter discussion of Disneyland is evidence.

To expose Baudrillard's use of simulation, I turn now to the constructs previously mentioned, "the three orders of simulacra," which encapsulate Baudrillard's critical method.

In its broadest sense, Baudrillard uses the term of simulacra to mean cultural sign systems that present an *appearance* or a *likeness as reality;* these appearances organize sociocultural life. Simulacra present a reality principle with categories that determine how society understands itself and its environment. These categories are a *representation* or self-image of the society itself, informing and unifying each sphere of society, making it into a cohesive whole.[6] And, simulacra regulate institutional practices in ways that seek to reproduce and perpetuate the *status quo*. But, simulacra evolve historically.

Indeed, Baudrillard's three orders of appearance designate historical epochs with correlative techniques of production and value. The first order of simulacra designates the Renaissance, the second order refers to the Industrial epoch, and the third order corresponds to the Postindustrial time period.

The Renaissance begins and industrial capitalism ends the first-order simulacrum. The sign of the epoch is the counterfeit. Things are handcrafted counterfeits; they emulate the forms of nature. And, following the law of the human metabolism with nature, use-value regulates the economy; that is, objects are made to satisfy immediate needs.[7] The referential power of the *signifier/signified* couplet is shown in the handmade object as artifice/nature, product/use-value, and product/living labor.

The modern period of industrial capitalism is the second order simulacrum. Its sign is the machine, which introduces technique: the production of a series of two or of "n identical things."[8] Nature, use-value, and the human artisan drop out and are replaced by the commodity-form of equivalence. Commodities gain significance not as material objects but as *signifiers,* whose value is measured against exchange with other commodities. And, in the commodity form, human labor itself appears transformed into the equivalence of the dead labor of wages. In Baudrillard's words, technique means that as "objects are transformed into simulacra of one another . . . so are the people who produce them. [This] extinction of original human reference permits the law of equivalence [and] the possibility of production."[9]

---

[6]   See B.G. Chang, "Mass Media, Mass Mediation: Jean Baudrillard's Implosive Critique of Modern Mass-Mediated Culture," *Current Perspectives in Social Theory VII* (1986): 157–181.

[7]   K. Marx, *Capital Vol. I*, trans. Ben Fowkes (London: Penguin Books, 1976), 283–284.

[8]   J. Baudrillard, "Orders of Simulacra," in *Structuralism: An Introduction*, ed. D. Robey (London: Oxford University Press, 1972), 63.

[9]   Ibid.

The postmodern period of information technology is the third-order simulacrum. Its sign system is the simulation. Its vehicles, the computer and electronic media, revolutionize the structure of representation. If the first-order simulacrum counterfeited reality and second order simulacrum made human beings and products appear as commodities, the third-order simulacrum of the hyper-real makes the question of the adequacy of the sign system to any preexisting referent nonsensical. That is, the hyper-real is a radical new order of things because it produces a simulation without a referent in the real world.[10] The prior division between sound image/concept and thing, or *signifier* and *signified,* disappears. Further, the replication of the real by another medium, and even the distinction between real and the medium, is gone. Its replacement is a phantom content in which the real and the medium appear as one.[11] Baudrillard's argument must not be taken simplistically to mean that all experience in contemporary society is hyper-real or loaded with symbols having no referents. Baudrillard instead is looking at imagery in art, electronic media, advertisements, and recreational activities that deliver messages that are ideological. Such messages are bound up with, summarize, and reinforce the socioeconomic system and its values. These representations are signs without referents, if what is simulated presents as historical reality a value or event that is more apparent than real. An example is the depiction of the ideology of equal opportunity for all, regardless of race, sex, or gender, or the simulation intermixing simulacra of different historical epochs. I will show this is the case later in the Dewey occupational model.

Put differently, the hyper-real is a simulation beyond the truth and monetary exchange value. The hyper-real copies nothing. Its *signifiers* are not equivalent to money. The value structure of the hyper-real is one of commutation; each *signifier's* value is equivalent to that of any other *signifier within the simulation.* Each s*ignifier signifies* only itself; each *signified* is its own referents. Baudrillard calls this phenomenon an implosion of meaning in which reality loops around itself. What we accept are the simulated effects of the real world's absence. To fill this

---

[10]   Ibid., 71.
[11]   B.G. Chang, "Mass Media, Mass Mediations," 162.

absence, simulations often resurrect imagery and messages from the past. This hyper-reality is a fabrication of image and imaginary. It presents an imagined, fictive real, seemingly more real and more appealing than reality itself.

Consider Disneyland as a paradigm case of the hyper-real. The venue, Adventureland Liberty Square, is illustrative. The Disneyland brochure describes Adventureland as a jungle cruise where one can "explore untamed lands and waterways, where elephants, hippos, tigers and snakes threaten at every bend."[12]

Adventureland is an Africa made for American consumption, a place without a history. The twentieth century realities of famine and political revolutions are absent. Certainly this is not a copy of anything real. In place of the real, Adventureland is the tropical rainforest in "living Technicolor."[13] This is a new and improved, primeval Africa, a place of tranquil ferocity, where wild beasts scare the customers, yet still seem cute. This is the spectacle of real animals appearing as inflated rubber beasts, lolling on a field so green it gleams, like plastic. Adventureland is the pacified naturescape of Henri Rousseau made into a kitsch never-never land.

On the surface, the introduction of Disneyland as a paradigm of the *hyper-real* seems a bad choice. Disneyland seems only to be an instance of larger-than-life entertainment, allowing visitors detachment from the pressures of everyday life. Indeed, for the adult, Disneyland appears as a huge diorama—an environment where viewers become participants in a staged event. No political significance is apparent here. But, ironically, this is exactly why Disneyland is a good choice. Disney's Africa is a place without famine, political turmoil, race, hatred, and death. Disneyland expresses the hyper-real as part of the taken-for-granted world. This is an uncomplicated world of harmony that we can only wish for. In this sense, Disneyland, like other examples of the hyper-real, works like a dream: the hyper-real is experience made more real than the real. Why? Because this is a depoliticized, atemporal world of wish-fulfillment.

---

[12]   *Disneyland* (Los Angeles: Walt Disney Corporation, 1972).
[13]   Ibid.

Keeping Baudrillard's constructs of three orders of simulacra in mind, I want to shift to a description of Dewey's views on the schoolroom simulations of occupations, looking first at connections to mind and method. I have chosen Dewey's occupational simulation for three reasons. First, it was the central theme in speeches he gave to parents in describing the workings of the University of Chicago laboratory. Second, all schools in Dewey's time and our own perform the ideological function of inculcating cultural values and forming the child. Finally, Dewey's simulation of occupations (with some necessary changes) is extremely attractive to educators, even today.

Dewey's notion of mind signals the technique of reconstituting human experience; to act with a mind is to control, enhance, and preserve experience so that more and qualitatively better experience can follow. Mind is not a thing, but a sense-giving operation; mind is the operation of human intelligence in the world, and means a consideration of the facts of a situation, including a consideration of what has to be done, a review of the relationship means and ends, an anticipation of the present and future consequences of a plan of action, and the execution of that idea to secure an end-in-view.

Of course, Dewey's analysis rejects the Cartesian *cogito,* an immaterial, private entity set against the materiality of an outside world and body. The *cogito* denies our ordinary experience of the world. Instead, it describes mind as "complete in each person and isolated from nature and hence from other minds. But [Dewey argues] when men act, they act in a common and public world."[14] This is not to say the simple recognition of the public nature of mind is enough. Dewey argues that many educationists fail because they ignore the need to set up the proper environmental context of teaching; they ignore the need to form the socialized mind. Dewey allows that the individual child must "have opportunity to employ his own powers in activities that have meaning. [But he insists] mind as a concrete thing is precisely the power to understand things in terms of the use made of them; a socialized mind is the power to understand them in joint or shared situations."[15]

---

14   J. Dewey, *Democracy and Education* (New York: MacMillan, 1916), 297.
15   Ibid., 33.

96

The above description sets down direction for the classroom formation of mind. The prior question, however, concerns the need to develop a method that connects to the child's real nature. Put differently, any talk about forming the mind is useless, unless and until the teacher actually makes use of the child's native powers or tendencies. Dewey calls these native tendencies instincts or impulses, and he couples the exercise of these instincts to the child's classroom simulation of adult occupations. Before describing this simulation, it is necessary to consider Dewey's view of the instinctual nature of the child.

At the outset, Dewey contextualizes the discussion about instincts and their proper exercise with the claim that the school must be changed over into the ideal home. This means first, that the teacher must act like "the parent who is intelligent enough to recognize what is best for the child, and is able to supply what is needed."[16] Dewey then lists the child's instincts under four headings: the social-conversational, the making or constructive, the inquiry, and the expressive or aesthetic instinct.

In exercising the social instinct, classroom recitation and attendance competition are replaced with free and active social intercourse between peers and teacher. The child raises "points of interests and value to him in the conversation carried on; statements are made, inquiries arise, topics are discussed, and the child continually learns."[17]

The constructive instinct describes the child's impulse to use the hands and to manipulate things. Dewey says that the natural outlet of this tendency is "in shaping materials into tangible forms and permanent embodiment."[18] His example is of a child who constructs a box. In the process of making plans, using tools to saw, plane, sandpaper, and joint the pieces of wood together, the child embodies problem-solving activity. The inquiry instinct combines both the constructive and conversational instincts, and previews the abstract investigations of chemistry and physics. His example is of children determining the effects that various degrees of water temperature produce on the white of an

---

[16] J. Dewey, *The Child and the Curriculum* (Chicago: University of Chicago Press, 1900, 1956), 34.

[17] Ibid., 35.

[18] Ibid.

egg.[19] The aesthetic instinct appeals to the children's desire to make something and to "give it a social motive, something to tell . . . a work of art."[20] His example is of a classroom of children who build a primitive loom and then weave blankets modeled on a Navajo Indian design.

As I have already indicated, the medium that integrates the instincts with the formation of mind is the child's simulation of adult occupations. There is a manifold appeal in these simulations: occupations provide intrinsic interest, are joined to the instincts, embody the thinking process, and recapitulate the history of the race. Dewey defines occupations as "a mode of activity on the part of the child which reproduces, or runs parallel to, some form of work carried on in social life."[21]

Unlike actual work though, the simulation of occupations is not work for pay; instead, classroom occupations are "an end in themselves [and their purpose is to develop] . . . the [child's] mental and moral states [as well] as the growth involved in the process of reaching a result."[22] As I have already noted, Dewey claims that occupations are interesting because they grow out of instincts. His evidence is the spontaneous interest the child demonstrates in play outside of school. That play involves haphazard attempts to reproduce social occupations. That play not only gives an outlet to the instincts, it repeats the never ending effort of the race to master the force of nature, "through [the] getting of food to maintain life; securing clothing to protect and ornament it, and thus finally, to provide a permanent home."[23] Quite simply, the juncture of instincts and the simulation of occupations represent the human's fundamental relations to the world.

A closer look at the Dewey texts reveal why and how all of this is to be done. At bottom, Dewey argues that the classroom simulation of occupations does two things: first, the experience of children working together on an interesting task which demands practical thinking converts dead subject matter into a living reality; secondly, the roles that the child simulate represent an accurate picture of the adult world and

[19]   Ibid., 39.
[20]   Ibid., 44.
[21]   Ibid., 132.
[22]   Ibid., 134.
[23]   J. Dewey, *Democracy and Education*, 199.

human progress. In *Democracy and Education,* Dewey sets down a list of available occupations and comingled processes. The children there:

> Work with paper, cardboard, wood, leather, cloth, yarns, clay and sand, and the metals with and without tools. [Processes employed] are folding, cutting, pricking, measuring, molding . . . and the operations characteristic of such tools as the hammer, saw, and file. Outdoor excursions, gardening, cooking, sewing . . . weaving [all forms what he calls] active pursuits with social aims.[24]

His essay, "The School and Social Progress," describes the children's recapitulation of the processes that convert raw materials into cloth. Using "raw wool as it comes from the back of the sheep [they] reinvent the first frame for the carding of wool—a couple of boards with sharp pins in them. They redevised the simplest process for spinning wool . . . [a] weight through which the wool is passed" is then twirled to draw out the fiber.[25]

Unlike the teacher-centered classroom in which children are given prescriptions and dictation—a place in which they reproduce ready-made models, here the children have something to do. In the simulation of occupations, "appliances are brought to bear on physical things with the intention of effecting useful changes [and this] is the most vital introduction to the scientific method."[26] Put differently, what the children directly experience are not only the practical applications of chemistry, physics, and reading—ideas hidden in textbooks—but also the test of those ideas, directly in the real world. Dewey refers to this activity as thinking.

While my intent has been to present the salient features of Dewey's pedagogy of occupations, what remains is the need to reexamine the text to discover the overarching moral purpose of these simulations. Dewey's moral argument follows these three lines.

First, today (1915) we live in a social world in which every phase of life has been profoundly changed by the effects of the factory system of industrial capitalism:

---

24   Ibid., 196.
25   J. Dewey, *The Child and the Curriculum,* 21.
26   J. Dewey, *Democracy and Education,* 202.

Books, magazines, papers were multiplied and cheapened. As a result of the locomotive and telegraph, frequent, rapid, and cheap intercommunication by mails and electricity was called into being . . . freedom of movement with . . . exchange of ideas, indefinitely facilitated. Learning has been put into circulation . . . actively moving in all the currents of society itself.[27]

Second, the change from hand production in the home to machinery production in the factory has also produced profound socioeconomic changes, and many of these changes are negative. For example, the face-to-face interdependent work of the family in the household system demanded a rational socialized experience. All of the processes needed to master nature and sustain life stood revealed. What was produced was something immediately necessary—a product having *use-value*. And, what was produced in the child was a moral conscience that came from seeing one's place and purposes in a genuine community life.

"We cannot overlook the factors of discipline and of character guiding in this kind of life . . . something to be done . . . a real necessity that each member of the household should do his own part faithfully and in cooperation with others."[28] But, the negative side of industrial capitalism is that the machine has also transformed life into something mean and nasty. The factory worker is subordinated into the rhythms of the machine.

The mechanical processes of the machine itself hide the activities of production—the conversion of raw material into a product of use-value made by hand disappears. This absence ushers a dramatic economic and social dislocation. As the things stamped out by the machine become commodities, the worker labors only for money. Appearing to self as identical and replaceable as the things made by machine, she or he becomes alienated from others. Dewey recognizes in the consciousness of the worker the sense of being only an "appendage to the machine." He likens this to the condition of slavery: "Plato somewhere speaks of the slave as one who in his actions does not express his own ideas, but those of some other. It is our social problem now . . .that method, purpose,

---

[27]   J. Dewey, *The Child and the Curriculum*, 25.

[28]   Ibid., 11.

understanding, shall exist in the consciousness of the one who does the work, that his activity shall have meaning to himself."[29]

Third, Dewey's solution is to have the schools catch up with the "general march of events" by recapturing the familial cooperation of the household system. His moral purpose is to set in place an embryonic community of democratic living. With this in mind, I shall return to the critique of Dewey's simulation. To begin, I want to reassert the obvious: Dewey is a philosopher who wants to change the culture. I see him as one who believes that the experience and values instantiated in the classroom form the possibility of a truly democratic society. But, for Dewey and his times, democracy was a way of living that had not been realized—a review of his articles in the *Social Frontier* of the 1930s shows that.

To answer the question, "Why does the simulation of occupations fail?", the fundamental answer is that Dewey's simulation fails to recognize the political significance of the shift from the counterfeit or first order to that of the second order industrial capitalist epoch. What are the implications here? Remembering that Baudrillard has assimilated and revised the Marxist critique into structuralist terms, and that Dewey's pedagogy mirrors Marx's distinction between *use-value* and *exchange-value*, my critique uses Marxist thematics within the Baudrillard context. A review of Baudrillard's categories is helpful. This fundamental epistemological misrecognition is built on three concepts.

First, Dewey's simulation does not illustrate the economic change of the industrial revolution—a change in value from that of *use-value* to *exchange-value* fundamentally altered sociopolitical relationships. The counterfeit, or first-order simulacrum, emphasized that the product was hand crafted. The value of the product was determined by humans. With the machine culture and commodity production, the value of a thing is determined by other things: the commodity is measured against another thing, gold, and that value fluctuates according to the law of supply and demand. Again, human living labor power is made equivalent to money, and the human is transformed into a commodity.

Second, Dewey's simulation separates the social form of life from its

---

[29] Ibid., 23.

social content. The household production relationship is one of mutual interdependence for survival. The object produced reflects those who created it. But, the worker in the industrial capitalist simulacrum fails to see an objectification of self in work. The relationship of worker to factory owner is a class, adversarial relationship.

Finally, Dewey's simulation actually psychologizes the political reality of class differences.[30] When the use of occupational simulations is used in the school so that the future industrial worker may see "the social value of his work," the source of the worker's alienation is hidden. Again, that source lies in the worker's actual production relationship in the industrial epoch. The attempt to resurrect the moral characterology of the household economy and to graft it onto the industrial economy is unreal. But, if the misrecognition of the industrial capitalist simulacrum turned Dewey's purposes inside out, the use of the occupation technique in the postmodern classroom both exacerbates that political condition and illustrates the notion of hyper-reality.

Ironically, the occupation technique appears specially tailored for the postmodern epoch. Calculators, computers, and word processors are now the rule in the teaching of the three "R's": television also is a co-equal partner in telling children about the world.

And this is precisely the trouble; these aids have once again isolated children and made them passive. The tedious work of long division or the parsing of a sentence is what the child passes on to the computer. In fact, for some children the work of getting knowledge might be reduced to shuffling bits of information shown on a monitor. It seems to make sense, then, to return to Dewey's "occupation" technique. *The simulation appears to deliver the right kind of practical, social, and moral experience without any mediation*—the lesson is lived by the child directly.

Today, to choose Dewey's technique of occupations is to choose the hyper-real. A familiar example of the hyper-real, that of Andy Warhol's pop art, works well to underscore similarities with Dewey's technique.

---

[30] Dewey's stipulative use of the term "psychologize" denotes the deliberate attempt to adapt classroom pedagogy in ways that connect to the child's experiences outside of the school, in the home, and in the neighborhood.

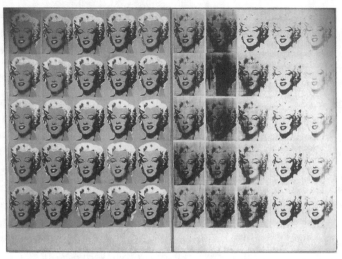

Andy Warhol, "Marilyn Monroe Diptych," 1962.
© 2001 Andy Warhol Foundation for the Visual Arts/ARS, New York.

The Warhol imagery of "Brillo Boxes," "Campbell Soup Cans," or "Marilyn Monroe" is public imagery repeated. This is the stuff of advertisements. We are so saturated by these images, they are so pervasive, so unrelenting, and so trite, that they appear *natural;* that is, they seem always to have been part of the culture. Consequently, we no longer really see them. Warhol forces us to pay attention, by simulating, exaggerating, and repeating these banalities. His favorite device is to repeat the same images on a grid. "Marilyn Monroe," for instance, is a work that features the actress' image twenty-five times: the same image of her face is reproduced in five rows across and five rows down. Warhol was demanding that we break the chain of looking without seeing, by placing the act of repetitive looking into a new medium.[31]

But, more importantly, Warhol was playing both with the machine technique of industrial capitalism (the production of a series of two or of "n" identical things) and the counterfeit objects. That is, the painting "Marilyn Monroe" combines elements of both the second and first

---

[31] E.B. Feldman, *Art as Image and Idea* (Englewood Cliffs: Prentice-Hall., Inc. 1967), 336.

simulacra. But unlike the second-order value structure of industrial capitalism, Warhol's "painting as a painting" has no real referent. It is not, for example, a piece of advertisement meant to generate a real audience for a Monroe movie. Likewise, the painting is not even a likeness of the real woman "Monroe"; it is not a counterfeit. "Marilyn Monroe" is a monumentalized banal image in which the *signifier/signified* couplet become one. This "Marilyn Monroe" expresses the *hyper-real*.

In what sense is the Dewey simulation for today's children like the Warhol example, the hyper-real? Dewey's specific example of the children's reenactment of the process of changing raw wool into fiber is illustrative. Dewey tells the reader how the children reinvented a simple frame for carding the wool and of another device to spin it. Like Warhol, the teacher who uses "occupations" resuscitates a message located within popular culture. For the teacher, that message is "Dewey's philosophy is, 'We learn by doing!'" The reinvention of the frame is an attempt to have children look again, to have them see the hidden processes of production. Like Warhol, the teacher revives an icon from the past (in this instance a machine) and a way of life that has disappeared. But what really is being simulated here?

The answer is nothing. The frame is not a copy of something real. The labor relationships acted out do not exist in the real world: the occupations expressed are depoliticized and ahistorical. The social relationships describe life as we would dream them; they are examples of wish-fulfillment. This is an agrarian utopia, more fun and more humane than our experience of the world. This simulation wants to represent to children how we would see ourselves—what Baudrillard has called a simulacrum. In fact, it is the simulacrum of our age—the hyper-real, which represents the fetishism of a lost object, an absence that is simulated.[32] The children's reinvention of the frame works precisely that way. The democratic style of conjoint living that is simulated is the living image of an imaginary past. Such an experience is absent from, and a denial of, today's real life. Dewey's simulation, like Warhol's

---

[32]   K. Linker, "From Imitation to the Copy of Just Effect: On Reading Jean Baudrillard," in *Art Form* (April, 1984): 46.

painting, is complete onto itself. Without a referent in the world, the occupation technique signifies only itself. In other words, for today's students Dewey's pedagogy of occupations is caught within its own simulations loop.

Now, it would be wrong to conclude from all of this that I think that Dewey's work is outdated or wrongheaded. Quite the contrary, my belief is that Dewey was the single most important philosopher of education that America has produced. My caveat is simply this: if one today would like to implement Dewey's occupational simulation in the schools, the first task is to ask how these pedagogical techniques reflect the real world.

A final word regarding Baudrillard. My use of his critical apparatus has been restricted to examining the impact of simulacra on a specific pedagogy. I find his criticisms of Foucault on power and Kristeva on postfeminism highly controversial. Space does not permit a lengthy response, other than to say Baudrillard's attack previews the development of a Grand Narrative. The latter move works against the intent of this book. Baudrillard's description of hyper-reality evidences a self-reflexive criticism of the sources of his own critical apparatus. Saussure, Marx, and Foucault are either assimilated or rejected. Saussure's semiological methodology is assimilated as Baudrillard privileges the symbolic exchange of social life, but the location of a real referent drops out. Marx's separation of use value and exchange-value is collapsed into social values that are all differentiated symbolically in a consumer world. Finally, Baudrillard asks that we *Forget Foucault,* because Foucault still labors under the impression that we can unravel electronic mediations and reach the hard copy of the world.

Chapter Seven shifts to the issue of racism and the school's response to it—namely multicultural curricula. An application of Jacques Derrida's poststructuralist techniques offers a different reading of the school's formation of subjectivity. Derrida applies and critiques the phenomenological themes of temporality, subjectivity, and the work of language.

Chapter 7
Derrida:
Reading Racism
and Cultural Pluralism

The readings in this chapter apply Jacques Derrida's constructs of *différance* and *supplement*. In the first section, *différance* is joined together with the ontology of the existential phenomenologist, Jean-Paul Sartre, and the aesthetic of the pop artist Jasper Johns, to expose the metaphysical principle of racism.

The second section moves to a multicultural model of pedagogy, cultural realism, and finds this discourse to be an expression of White, Anglo-Saxon, Protestant, ethnocentrism.

A pedagogy that deals with racism would best follow Dewey's advice that the teacher must psychologize the material. That is, connect curriculum to the student's "own past doings, thinkings and sufferings."[1] The implication: attempts at multicultural education must first read and decipher the racist text of the student's lived experience. In the first

---

[1]   John Dewey. "The Child and the Curriculum," in *The Child and the Curriculum and the School and Society* (Chicago: The University of Chicago Press, 1971), 200.

section, selected works taken from Johns, Sartre, and Derrida are used to psychologize the language of racism and to ground an interventionist model. The intent is to expose the invisible palpability of racism as a metaphysical principle that directs cultural life. I use the term "metaphysical" to mean an essence, i.e., a historical fixed political reality that reifies understanding the other.

To claim that racism is an invisible palpability is to argue that racism is a social form of life, so pervasive that we do not see it; when it speaks to us, we may be unaware of its hold.

The task of the first section is to treat racism from opposing philosophical perspectives, to use accessible texts and to expose the reader to alternative ways of seeing. The texts chosen are the artist Jasper Johns' painting, "Flag," Jacques Derrida's article, *Racism's Last Word,* and Jean-Paul Sartre's *Anti-Semite and Jew.* Each text is used to expose how a racist semiotics directs the culture. But more than that, they expose a different way of dealing with racism—a range of strategies from the preverbal to the linguistic that allow the reader to see himself/herself.

Although each of these works differ, each reveals the aim of disrupting a commonly shared social construction of experience. The model that emerges is an aesthetic of *différance.*

To lay the groundwork of this aesthetic, the analysis begins with Johns, whose work expresses a shift in the artistic idiom from the modern to the postmodern. If Jackson Pollock's canvas assaulted the viewer with frenetic lines of force and bold striations of color that punched the viewer into a state of *angst,* so be it. Pollock, the icon of modernism, embodied the ethic of a unique vision, self-expression, and the *avant-garde* quest for spiritual purity.[2] For most, however, modernism was a private language inaccessible and untranslatable.

Against this, Johns' postmodernist paintings are filled with representations of real things: numbers, flags, maps, even noses. The subject matter appears lifted directly from ordinary life; it is at once recognizable, banal, derivative, and recycled. Moreover, his work seems not so much an instance of unique self-expression as the anonymous, jumbled sensibility of Everyman: the portraiture of Kodak instamatic: spiritual *angst* is replaced by profane humor. The 1958 Johns canvas, "Flag," is a paradigm case, which depicts the American flag on three

---

[2]   Rosalind E. Krauss, "Split Decisions, Jasper Johns in Retrospect," *Art Forum* 35, no. 3 (1996): 79.

Jackson Pollock, "Lavender Mist: Number 1," 1950.
© 2001 The Pollock-Krasner Artists Rights Society (ARS), New York

wooden panels, using the medium of wax encaustic.[3] The stars appear like cutouts, which are stuck to the surface crust. But, unlike "The Stars and Stripes," Johns' flag is a stiff, flat, thick simulacrum. It certainly looks like the flag, but we know it at once as a reproduction: this flag cannot and was never meant to fly.

What is going on then? In Johns' words: I begin with "things the mind already knows. I like to repeat an image in another medium to observe the play between the two, the image and the medium." One way to make sense of Johns' distinction is to *treat both flags as signs* and then contrast the opposing significations. Begin with the real flag and ask what you already know. From my own experience, what I already know is that in kindergarten I mouthed allegiance to, and in the United States Marine Corps I saluted, the flag. The lesson was that the flag is a patriotic sign, something that stands for me and all Americans. But what is hidden in these prosaic observations is a cultural narrative sending certain political, emotional, and spiritual messages. Politically, a pledge of allegiance to the flag denotes acceptance of the authority of the government. One also already knows such a pledge acknowledges the possibility (if not the likelihood) of being conscripted. Spiritually, the flag signifies the renewal of the nation as it is taken up by each generation. What the American already knows then, is that the flag is an icon with a message: the flag says, "You are an American citizen."

The Johns "Flag" is a material contradiction. The painting "Flag" is

---

3   Robert Hughes, *The Shock of the New* (New York: Alfred A. Knopf, 1991), 340.

108

also not a flag; the viewer experiences the painting now as a political trope and again as an artistic design. Stated simply, Johns has put the sign of the flag into spasm. Like an involuntary contraction, Johns' "Flag" breaks down the one "true" set of meanings that pairs the sign "American Flag" with the signified citizenship. Significations are split. Johns' flag is no longer a surrogate for patriotism; it is simultaneously an aesthetic object that at once intrudes on and cancels perceptions, defers original significations, and produces a play of signs.

The beauty in this is that Johns' canvas has represented a quasi-sacred sign taken from ordinary life and broken the metaphysical chain; that is, the fixed one-to-one correspondences between the flag and patriotic behaviors. Johns' flag collides against the fixed patriotic ensemble of signifier/signified in a new, different, and disruptive system. Saluting Johns' "Flag" is more than inappropriate; such a performative is an "unnatural act."

The critic Christopher Knight argues that Johns' work created a vacuum that showed how works of art attain notice, stature, and even meaning: they represent the interests of like-minded individuals, drawn from among a differentiated public that constitutes the audience. The authority of social experience, materialized through an artistic language of idiosyncratic private pleasure, is what characterized Johns' surprising work, not the other way around.[4] Put simply, the "Flag" painting, when viewed as an abstract aesthetic form, "displaces social usage into a new context. [The result is that a singular unquestioned] social function ceases."[5]

Doubtless, Johns did not intend "Flag" as an aesthetic critique of racism. But the power of Johns' "Flag" to change the viewer's consciousness is echoed in Derrida's deconstruction of metaphysical language.

A brief discussion of the latter is illustrative. Derrida radicalized Ferdinand Saussure's discovery that language is built on the differences between signifier and signified, insisting that signifiers produce a signification without precise origin. Most important, the metaphysical misuse of language begins with the speaker's elision of the difference between signifier and signified. That is, the speaker is under the delusion of having direct access to thought, and that his/her word and thought are

[4]   Christopher Knight, "Split Decisions, Jasper Johns in Retrospect," *Art Forum* 25, no. 3 (1996): 84.
[5]   Ibid.

Jasper Johns, *Flag*, 1954-1955.
© Jasper Johns/Licensed by VAGA, New York, NY.

a transparency. Moreover, this mistake presents language in essentialist terms as a substance that appears to the speaker as unmediated. Derrida says, "[this] auto affection is experienced as a suppression of difference—this phenomenon, this presumed suppression of difference, this lived reduction of the opacity of the signifier, are the origin of what we call presence."[6]

The source of this mistaken presence is the sound of one's own voice: "this priority of the signified leads back to a putative grounding in speech and self-presence . . . it identifies consciousness itself with the absolute privilege granted to vocal expression . . . such is at least the experience—or consciousness of the voice: of hearing (understanding) oneself speak."[7]

This blindness to the difference between content and representation (that is, the difference between signifier and signified) submerges the fact that language, whether written or spoken, is built on a relationship of differences between marks and sounds, differences in spelling, pronunciation, and definition, and differences between context and parts of speech.

Derrida emphasizes that the consequence of treating speech as self-presence is the negative assessment of writing as the inferior, subordinate

6 Jacques Derrida, *Of Grammatology*, trans. Gayatri Chakravorty Spivak (Baltimore: Johns Hopkins University Press, 1977), 166.
7 Ibid., 160.

110

supplement of speech. To overcome this blindness to the difference
between context and representation, Derrida reinstates the priority of
written language over spoken. He does this by recovering the exterior
public, spatial signifier interrupting self-presence.

This priority of writing tears apart the self-identity of signifier and
signified, by emphasizing what Derrida calls *différance*. Obviously,
différance also is a new spelling of the French *difference,* meant to
underscore the difference between writing and speech. *Différance* means
both to differ in meaning and to defer meaning. *Différance* points to the
impossibility of locating the absolute origin of language in either event
or structure.

Différance refers to the impossibility of locating a pure temporal
punctum, a present point in time experienced without the overlap and
difference of past and future that frame the present. But the key is that
différance points to the breakup of metaphysical self-presence and
destroys the pretense of absolute closure in language.[8]

To summarize the above, the connective tissue between Johns and
Derrida is that of *différance*. Obviously, each is working with different
texts: artistic artifacts as against words. But, "Flag" first defers and then
displaces an original, seemingly natural, and permanent signified. "Flag"
also exposes the protean possibilities of the sign system. In both Derrida
and Johns, this difference breaks up self-presence and denies any text the
possibility of an ultimate meaning.

The technique I have used to compare Derrida and Johns is what the
deconstructionist calls "grafting." A "graft" is the production of a new
structure in which two side-by-side but separate discourses are sewn
together. Derrida compares grafting to the act of "passing a knife
between two texts." And he asks, "Why do it? Or at least why write two
texts at once?"[9]

The answer is that making sense of one text depends on the
examination of the second text. Put differently, reading the second text
reverses the meaning of the first text by exposing contradictions within
it, exposing metaphysical closures.

Derrida's critique of the metaphysics of racism is of the latest form
of twentieth century racism, the apartheid system of South Africa.
Derrida's piece, "Racism's Last Word," was written in 1983 (before the

---

[8] Jacques Derrida, *Positions* (Chicago: University of Chicago Press, 1981).
[9] Jacques Derrida, *Writing and Difference*, trans. Alan Bass (London: Rutledge and
Kegan Paul, 1978), 126.

Mandelan Revolution) as a commentary for the UN exhibition of paintings, "Art Contra Apartheid." "Racism's Last Word" is a philosophical critique that excavates the double-bind logic of the law of apartheid.[10] Throughout that piece, Derrida treats apartheid as a watchword asking the questions: "What do the discourses of apartheid say?" And, "How are the claims that rationalize apartheid contradicted by their own proofs?" Thus is a deconstruction of the text of apartheid; in no sense is it an ordinary language exercise meant to unpack the use of the term. Derrida uses the term "text" to refer not simply to words on a page, but to the limits of situated real life. The text of apartheid demands action. Derrida's voice, then, is not declarative, but subjunctive and rhetorical.

However, Derrida's work goes beyond South Africa, revealing the metaphysics of self-presence that characterizes all racism. The critique is built on four themes: first, the metaphysics of the word "apartheid"; second, European discourse on race; third, theological-political discourse; finally, art as the negation of racism. His overarching concern is to reveal the moral contradictions that structure apartheid. My own analysis follows Derrida's technique of grafting. That is, two columns will be used to highlight the separate but independent texts found within apartheid.

First enacted as South African law in 1948, apartheid meant "the separate development of each race in the geographic zone assigned to it. [This meant] the forced assignment to 'natural' territory the geography of birth."

Apartheid is at once the name and the law. Because this duality is unrecognized, apartheid appears as a metaphysical essence. The graft of the texts exists between two columns.[11] The contradiction played between columns I and II reveals language used to hypostatize experience: the inexplicable nature of apartheid indicates that the term is a transcendental signifier—that is, a metaphysical self-presence that disallows other contents. And, the legal imperative of apartheid is legitimated by an appeal to origins—something not possible in the play of *différance*.

[10] Jacques Derrida, "Racism's Last Word," *Critical Inquiry* 12 (1985): 290–299.
[11] Ibid., 292.

112

Apartheid	
Column I: Word/Law	*Column II: Metaphysics*
Name and signifier in the Dutch	No signifier or equivalent in other languages
The signifier that marks separation (Heid), is an arrest mark.	Apartness appears ontological.
In the language of apartheid, racism is decreed natural.	Legitimation appears to be a creationist, divine law.

The significance of Johns' "Flag" for all of this is underscored in the 1964 apartheid law that forbade blacks even to touch the flag of the South African Republic. For example, the South Africa's Ministry of Public Works sought to assure the 'cleanliness' of national emblems by means of a regulation stipulating that it is forbidden for non-Europeans to handle them. This censorship of touch symbolized in the handling of the flag signifies that the black citizen owes obedience to the republic. Simultaneously, his/her touch with whites must be erased as unclean. In this contradiction, the black is no longer human, but a disembodied, disenfranchised cipher. Unfortunately, the European discourse on apartheid appears as counterfeit: moral denunciations against apartheid are voiced even as the West protects the Praetorian government. The most powerful declaration in the 1973 United Nations pronouncement declared apartheid "a crime against humanity." But Derrida exposes contradictory oppositions between this ideological language of the West and the political reality.[12]

However, the most hellish aspects of apartheid are legitimated, as theology is made to turn tricks, and scripture serves as the handmaiden of politics. The contradictions are internal as theological discourse is grafted to the politics of separation and control.[13]

In the end, Derrida provides incisive conclusions regarding apartheid, America, and thinking itself. First, he believed the double-bind logic legitimating apartheid had won. Against the indictment by Amnesty International that "As long as apartheid exists, there can be no structure conforming to generally recognized norms of human rights and able to guarantee their application," he sees the worn-out ideological homilies

---

[12] Ibid., 292.
[13] Ibid.

once again used to legitimatize this repression. For example: "world peace, the general economy, the marketplace for European labor all would be threatened by Western intervention to end apartheid."[14]

European Discourse	
Signifier	*Signified*
Western Ideology The myth: White migration preceded black migration into South	Political Reality Minority white population controls of government is legitimated.
White government, judicial superstructure—is just.	Racist regime has origins in Western culture—nature, life, history, religion, and law.
1973 Crime Against Humanity proclamation.	No Western nation acts to force abolition of apartheid. European trade with South Africa in gold and strategic ores is protected; the trade route around the Cape is open for trade in arms.

But most important for us, he finds America complicitous. In plain words, Derrida says, "Apartheid is surely an American problem." First, in an obvious sense, without an American decision to apply economic muscle, "especially in universities. Obliged to manage their capital," apartheid will continue.[15] But the real problem for America is its misreading of apartheid as a problem for South Africans, to be cured over there, by them. Apartheid, he claims, represents the segregation of American society: "No doubt, this segregation has become more urban, industrial, socioeconomic (the frightening percentage of young black unemployed, for example.)"[16] But the very need to speak this way to Americans, this need to expose racist ideology again and again underlines the failure of language itself. Derrida says that discourse, "draws contracts dialectizes itself and reappropriates again."[17]

Derrida searches for another mode of thinking to break through the prison-house of language. Like Johns, he finds it in art. While the

[14] Ibid., p. 295.
[15] Ibid.
[16] Ibid., p. 296.
[17] Ibid., p. 295.

immediate context is the exhibition that he is writing about, he draws larger conclusions about the "language" of art, citing Picasso's "Guernica" as a paradigm case.

The power of the exhibition derives from imagery. In this sense, the exhibition is like "Guernica"; it neither commemorates nor represents an event. "It is the name of hell, of a town and of a work." In place of words, "Guernica" fixes us with a "gaze that gazes back at us, making us its own object."[18]

Keeping in mind the connections between the ways metaphysical thinking is overcome by Johns and the application in Derrida's critique of apartheid, I shall now turn to Sartre. But before discussing his text, the need to show how to effect a legitimate misreading of Sartre, that is, one that shows a convergence with Derrida, must be dealt with. The early Sartre is an existential-phenomenologist, whose work is built on the intentionality of consciousness.[19]

Following this view, the human subject is described as *pour-soi,* incomplete and empty, a transcendence of the present moving toward a not yet. But, this free subjectivity is situated in the world of things: *en-soi,* full completions, as well as other persons. Being human means having to make choices without guaranteed outcomes. Living authentically means not avoiding, but bearing responsibility for, one's choices.

Denying choice, seeking relief from the contingency of freedom, indeed succumbing to the domination of the Other's freedom, involves the attempt by the subject to give up his/her freedom for the solidity and permanence of a thing. Such a metaphysical change is doomed to failure and represents inauthenticity. Freedom, choice, situation authenticity, inauthenticity, consciousness, *pour*-soi, and *en-soi* are the key words that structure *Anti-Semite* and *Jew*.[20]

Obviously, the problem in all of this is that Derrida's poststructuralist framework is a criticism of phenomenology. In place of the lived-world, one finds a text, instead of consciousness, the play of signifiers. Language then, not subjectivity, is where one begins to

---

18 Jacques Derrida, Critical Response *Critical Inquiry* 13, (1986): 155–170.

19 See especially Jean Paul Sartre, *Being and Nothingness*, trans. Hazel Barnes. (New York: The Citadel Press, 1968). pp. 420–421.

20 Robert Bernasconi, "Sartre's Gaze Returned, The Transformation of the Phenomenology of Racism," *Graduate Faculty Philosophy Journal* 18, no. 2 1995. 211.

investigate philosophy. Indeed, the notion of *différance* is meant to critique Husserl's model of time.[21]

Signifier	*Signified*
Theological Discourse Government has foundation in scripture; political power comes from God, who wants nations and people to be separate. The well-being of the colored man is central.	Political Implementation Prohibition of Mixed Marriage Act; reservation of separate amenities, population registration, segregates the races.
Equal educational opportunity The story of the Chosen People is found in the Long Trek. The *Bible* decrees that Whites should govern.	Institute for National Christian Education proscribed non-Christian or Marxists from teaching. Jews are excluded from government because of their own story. 72% of the population (black) is declared foreigners.

The question then becomes whether there is a link between Johns, Derrida, and Sartre. I believe the argument can be made by doing two things. First, the connection between aesthetic paradigms must be clarified. Second, and most importantly, the metaphysics of racism must be shown. This can be done by misreading *Anti-Semite and Jew,* and applying Derrida's grafting technique to key words and arguments within the text.

Sartre's aesthetic paradigm is encapsulated in a scene from his novel, *Nausea,* in which the protagonist, Roquentin, listens to a scratched recording of Bessie Smith singing "Some of These Days." Roquentin's response is this:

Behind the existent which tumbles from one moment to another, without past, without future, behind these sounds which decompose from day to day, are

---

21   Edmund Husserl, *The Phenomenology of Internal Time Consciousness.* trans. James S. Churchill, ed. Martin Heidegger (Bloomington: Indiana University Press, 1973), 48–49. Husserl develops the argument that temporal experience has an identifiable "source point."

chipped away and slide toward death, the melody remains the same, young and steady, like a witness without pity.[22]

Regarding literature itself, Sartre writes that literature requires "the conjoint effort of author and . . . reader . . . there is not art except for and by others."[23] The point is that the aesthetic object is cocreated by the artist and the sense-making activity of the "reader." Using different constructs, Sartre and Derrida come to the same conclusion. This is not a simple convergence, though. In reading the "Some of These Days" episode, what is obvious are Sartre's phenomenological concerns. Bessie Smith's words and the melody punctuate Roquentin's existence, by imposing order on the chaos of the character's life. More than that, "Some of These Days" is a phenomenological essence. That is, despite the record's scratches, Roquentin can play it again; he can return to a melody that is repeatable, unchanging, atemporal, and ideal.[24]

The convergence between Sartre and Derrida is found recalling the latter's discussion of "Guernica." In Derrida's words, "Guernica" neither commemorates nor represents an event . . . it is the name of hell, of a town and of a work."[25] Derrida reads this as a poststructuralist ideality. That is, the appeal is not to consciousness but to language. Displaced from its historical context of 1930s Spain, "Guernica" is a signifier in the imperative voice—the viewer is exhorted to move, overcome a present evil; "Guernica" is in the subjunctive mood—the viewer is reminded that South African freedom is a condition contrary to fact. "Guernica" highlights a past political repression in South Africa, and "Guernica" is a stimulus for a future free South Africa. Derrida named neither "Guernica" nor "Some of These Days" an ideality. The shared language, though, regarding the repetitive temporal signification of these aesthetic objects, as well as the cocreativity of artist-object-audience, marks a real convergence between both philosophers.

---

[22] Jean-Paul Sartre, *Nausea,* trans. Lloyd Alexander (New York: New Directions Publishing Corporation, 1964), 235.

[23] Jean-Paul Sartre, *What is Literature? And Other Essays,* trans. B. Frenchman. (Cambridge: Harvard University Press, 1988), 79–80.

[24] The irony here is double-edged: Sartre rejects Husserl's search for essences, emphasizing the transcendence of consciousness, and Derrida attacks Husserl's search for the *Arche* of consciousness in perception.

[25] Jacques Derrida, *Racism's Last Word,* 299.

Pablo Picasso, "Guernica." 1937
© 2001 Estate of Pablo Picasso/Artists Rights Society (ARS), New York.

This claim is reinforced when recalling Derrida's argument that "Guernica" fixes us with a gaze that "gazes back at us, making us its own object." This description could have been lifted out of *Being and Nothingness*. For Sartre, *le-regard* represents the stare of the other. The stare is the other's attempt to fix me in the present and transform me into Being for Others. Ironically, Derrida uses the gaze in his own way to overcome the metaphysical thinking of racism, just as Sartre's gaze jolts the reader to realize the existential demand of choice. In both examples, a profound *différance* overcomes metaphysical thinking. As in Johns' "Flag," both "Some of These Days" and "Guernica" are uprooted from a fixed signifier/signified correspondence. When caught in the loop of signification, the "reader" becomes more reflexive. That is, the signifier "Flag," and the Guernica paintings, and the record, "Some of These Days," are detached from a fixed meaning. The detached signifier floats, joined to other signifiers. The "reader" himself/herself becomes a signifier. What is crucial is that the reader is decentered and must respond.

In this context, *Anti-Semite and Jew* is read using Derrida's technique of grafting. The power in Sartre's text is more than any description of apartheid. His words hit us directly, illuminating racism by exposing the invidious racism in the heart. He says anti-Semitism is a racism which the anti-Semite can excuse in himself as simply a matter of his opinion, his personal choice and taste. But an opinion does not lend itself to criticism. Voicing an opinion closes a conversation, because what is really being said is, "This is what I think; don't try to change my mind; shut-up." Sartre's point, though, is that an "anti-Semitic opinion is the excuse to deprive Jews of their rights, to keep them out of economic and social activities, [even] to expel them from the country [and] exterminate them."[26] Certainly, Sartre is speaking about France of the 1950s. But his problem is our problem now, a metaphysical thinking that we can apply to ourselves, to our own situation. Sartre's attack on racist thinking is explicit: "If by race is understood the indefinable complex into which we are tossed pell-mell both somatic and intellectual moral traits, I believe in it no more than ouija boards."[27] Having said that, his focus is on anti-Semites' two systems of interpretation regarding "the idea of the Jew, the Jewish nature, and the Jewish role in society."[28] Indeed, the anti-Semite infuses his experience with hate founded in irrationality: the Jew is metaphysically bad, and the anti-Semite is the good citizen. The graft between these poles reveals an out-of-control passion. The issues of intelligence, citizenship, and human nature are illustrative.

The contradiction in all of this is obvious: human nature for Sartre is something we all share, only in the sense that, "the human is defined as a *being in situation*, a synthetic whole that is biological, economic, political and cultural. [Moreover, that situation] . . . is an ensemble of limits and restrictions: the necessity of working, sharing the world with others and death."[29] For the racist, the Jew is a metaphysical reality; she/he has an essence or substantial form which cannot be modified; she/he is free to do evil, but cannot do good.

This is the pretext the racist uses to color his experience. Sartre calls this person a symbolic murderer. He concludes that the anti-Semite "is a man who is afraid. Not of Jews . . . but of himself . . . of his liberty, of his instincts, of his responsibilities, of solitariness, of change, of society, and of the world—of everything except Jews."[30]

In Derrida's terms, the racist turns the Jew into a self-presence, a metaphysical signifier. The use of grafting rereads that lived text of racism, setting down its contradictions. The lesson is that the racist is

---

[26]   Jean-Paul Sartre, *Anti-Semite and Jew,* 7.
[27]   Ibid., 9.
[28]   Ibid., 61.
[29]   Ibid., 13.
[30]   Ibid., 23, 40, 80, 85, 113.

caught in the loop of fixed signification: he becomes the metaphysical signifier, unable to recognize the self-presence he has created.

Intelligence	
Jewish French Man	*"Native" French Man*
• In abstract, tentative deals with things such as money securities, and is destructive or critical. • Must earn his way, speaks a learned French that is acquired.	• Has a special sensibility, deals with the concrete, "is correct," and is magically connected to the land. • Inherits property, speaks the language with mistakes that are genius.
Citizenship	
Jewish French Man	*"Native" French Man*
• Government is Jew-ridden; • Jews vote in elections; • Authentic "Frenchness" is not available to him.	• Is above the law; • United in a social bond of anger, acquires French tradition, race, national destiny, has tact and a morality uniquely French, acquired at birth.
• If race does not exist, the Jew must have nothing to prove. Prove it. • Living contradiction: at once the rich Jewish Merchant is the agent of international capitalism and the Bolshevik.	• Is an ordinary worker.
Human Nature	
Jewish French Man	*"Native" French Man*
• Individual thinks, sleeps, eats is honest or dishonest, like a Jew. • Jewish way of speaking, reading, voting.	• Native sons and daughters enjoy • Has a culture not expressible in words.

There are several implications for the classroom; first, multicultural studies must deal with racism or become a sham. The idea that racism is someone else's problem must be attacked. This can be done by psychologizing racism, showing its lived everyday reality.

The above analysis of the metaphysics of racism needs translation into the everyday world of curriculum. Multicultural studies are the academy's response to the pervasive cultural malaise of racism, ethnocentrism, and the domination of women. The mandate is clear; cultural change is needed to overcome these inequities.

What is plainly obvious is that a myriad of competing multicultural paradigms have been offered which would change the structure and delivery of educational practices to respond to this need. But, intermixed in all of these models are competing definitions of ethnicity, gender, social class, and even political allegiance. I shall argue that making sense of multicultural education has as its first priority the political task of uncovering the racial and class bias insinuated within certain multicultural models, especially those named cultural pluralism.

In this context, and beginning with the premise that schooling is a political activity of social and self-formation, this section will begin with an examination of Diane Ravitch's model "Multiculturalism: *E Pluribus Plures*" as a form of cultural hegemony.[31] It will then move to a critique of Arthur Schlesinger's text, *The Disuniting of America*. Both texts are viewed as ideological statements that effectively deny recognition to American minority cultures, by presenting minorities as a supplement to the dominant WASP capitalist culture.

Of course, this description is stated too simply. Schlesinger is a prominent historian, who first was made famous to the lay public for his chronicle of John F. Kennedy's term as president of the United States. Ravitch is recognized in educational circles for her concern to improve American school curricula. This reading begins with the Ravitch article, to expose the ideological core of her cultural pluralism as a form of cultural hegemony. It then moves to specific arguments, such as the "melting pot" theory found in Schlesinger. The Ravitch article is a succinct presentation of the cultural pluralist position. After responding to her core argument, my reading of Schlesinger will employ Derrida's construct of the *supplement* to expose the ideological message of cultural pluralism.

---

[31] Diane Ravitch, "Multiculturalism: *E Pluribus Plures*," *Kaleidoscope: Readings in Education*, ed. Kevin Ryan and James Cooper (Houghton and Mifflin Co., 1992), 442–448.

Again, I begin with the premise that schooling is a political activity of social and self-formation. To put the Ravitch piece in context, I begin with the term "cultural hegemony." In this mystification, the real power relations within culture are hidden; class and race divisions seem nonexistent. Cultural hegemony works because it depoliticizes the social construction of reality by appealing to a definition of culture that has been called "Universalist Humanism." This Universalist Humanism is a representation found in cultural products and texts which delivers so-called "timeless and universal" values that span history and point to a cultural ideal. This representation is the fullness of an ethical model of the human; i.e., a universal human essence that transcends political differences, depicts developmental stages of becoming human, defines human freedom and authenticity, and is a model that the minority disenfranchised are to *mirror* in order to become empowered.

John Stuart Mill is an important source of this bourgeois political theory. *On Liberty* recognizes that a crucial problem of a large nation-state is that of the *need* for all groups within the state to *identify* as a collectivity. The minority person's allegiance and identity must supercede that of his/her group and reside in the nation. Mill's serious political definition of a minority is important, though, because a minority person's *position* is that of tutelage—human being who is developmentally *lacking*. Historically, this category means women, children, the disabled, and the insane. This ethnocentric model of culture legitimizes class division by demanding that the minority, working, and underclass assimilate the dominant culture's values, simultaneously disguise the minority class' denial of entrance to power. In all of this, opposing class interests are blunted and redefined as universal interests; and the minority's need to embrace this definition of things works to reinforce the political *status quo*.

Multiculturalism, when called cultural pluralism, is a case in point. The economic exploitation of Afro and Hispanic groups is reinforced, even as their ethnic differences from the dominant culture are tolerated. Specifically, I shall argue, the Ravitch argument shows all of the elements of hegemonic text: it depoliticizes the educational process, defines culture in Universalist terms, emphasizes the need for a national identity, and casts the multicultural education controversy in moral terms. The good is defined as cultural pluralism; evil is defined as cultural particularism.

122

At the outset, Ravitch acknowledges cultural divisions in the clash of what she calls "interest groups . . . who want to bring about fundamental social change."[32] Particularist interest groups are extremists who would redefine not only *how* but *what* should be taught in the schools. They are an irrational lot who would impose their views on teachers, cut off rational discussion, and politicize the educational process. Their ideas are bad and "are motivated by a political and professional interest in strengthening [their] ethnic power bases in the university, the education profession and in society."[33]

Cultural pluralists, on the other hand, speak for all interests. According to Ravitch, this group expresses the good and the correct thinking about multiculturalist education. They recognize cultural pluralism as "an ongoing principle of America . . . [a country with] a common culture formed by interaction of subsidiary cultures."[34] Indeed, these subsidiary cultures choose or have chosen for themselves whether to "maintain their cultural heritage or to assimilate.' All of this fits into Ravitch's Universalist definition of the task of the American public school. Namely:

(1) To create a national identity and a definition of citizenship,
(2) To not give preference to any racial or ethnic group,
(3) To teach children specific skills they need to function as American citizens, and
(4) To adhere to the principle of "*E Pluribus Unum*" – balancing the demands of the good of the whole against those of individual ethnic constituencies.

Against her cultural pluralist position, Ravitch sets down the negative agenda of the cultural particularists in these terms: Particularists,

(1) Find no common culture possible or desirable,
(2) Argue that the American culture is Eurocentered, implying those who are neither white nor European (in ancestry) are alienated, and

---

[32] Ibid., 442.
[33] Ibid., 444.
[34] Ibid., 443.

(3) Advocate a form of filiopietism, emphasizing that the identity of the minority person is determined by their "cultural genes."[35]

Ravitch argues that the Particularist scheme is overtly political and that its pedagogical consequences are absurd. In political terms, cultural particularism is seen as the recrudescence of separatist black nationalism; this ideology emphasizes the history of the white oppression of black Americans, promotes a minority ethnocentrism that papers over individual inadequacies, and simplistically categorizes all Americans along five discrete racial lines. She concludes that cultural particularism tends to find a home "in school districts where most children are black and Hispanic."[36] In pedagogical terms, Ravitch finds that cultural particularism is an absurdity; first, its ethnocentrism cannot hide the academic deficiencies of at-risk minority children. Second, it confuses the teacher who must teach minority children of mixed parentage. Third, it opens the possibility that each group will want to teach its own children in its own way. Fourth, it encourages the politicization of school curricula.

Beneath these seemingly apolitical descriptions, the arguments carry a political agenda that first appears in the binary opposition cultural pluralist/cultural particularist. Cultural pluralism is seen as the *rational* option championed by those who would preserve the common culture, uphold universal interests, reject discrimination, and equip all children to succeed in life. Indeed, Ravitch argues that the pluralists believe "American culture belongs to us, all of us."[37]

The major fallacy in the argument is that all groups share universal interests. The reality is that America is divided along class lines with competing political interests. What is most obvious to a person of color is the lie that assimilation is an organizing cultural principle. The opposite is most often the case. Indeed, the argument that cultural pluralists preserve a common culture is also false. Afro-Americans can point to a history of oppression in which their ancestral culture was systematically erased.

In the face of these realities, *Afrocentricity* has appeal to many Afro-Americans. But such a program she labels as cultural particularism. Although she does not name it explicitly, clearly this is what she has in

[35] Ibid.
[36] Ibid., 445.
[37] Ibid., 447.

mind as she describes cultural particularist curricula. Afrocentricity envisions a partitioned nation within the United States for all Afro-Americans. The ethnocentric dimension of the Afrocentric school curriculum replays the history of the oppression of Afro-Americans and recovers the origins of the black diaspora in the ancient Egypt of the pharaohs. Remember, Afrocentricity becomes a new way of life that constructs a new self: the Anglo name first foisted on one's slave ancestors is replaced with an African name; the white man's Christian religion is replaced by an African religion; and black pride promotes achievement. In sum, the racist White story is replaced with an African-American narrative of the black experience in the United States.

On the surface, Afrocentricity appears simplistic in its historiography, polarizing in its ethnocentrism, and simply dangerous in its politics. However, any literate American adult, not the victim of invincible ignorance, knows the facts: at the beginning of the twenty-first century, the conditions of life for working-class Afro-Americans have worsened. In this political context, I believe that Afrocentric "particularism" is the refracted image of cultural pluralism; moreover, cultural pluralism works to legitimize the *status quo*.

Cultural particularism, according to Ravitch, is a pernicious idea, for it is essentially an exercise in power politics. Once again, her own descriptions of particularist espouses a political definition of the American culture. There are several dimensions in her argument, but the master narrative on which all others turn is located in this sentence: "the unique feature of the United States is that its common culture has been formed by the interaction of its subsidiary cultures."[38] The obvious question is what constitutes a subsidiary culture? A subsidiary is a supplement, something added, secondary, and subordinate to another thing, which is original and preeminent. Tacitly understood here is that "particularist" subcultures within the United States supplement "original," dominant white Anglo-Saxon Calvinist culture and its secularized ethos, namely the capitalist social system. In fact, to say that this is an official ethnocentrism (one apparently without malice) risks bending the category, but also makes a point about forming children as Americans. It says to minorities: "A necessary condition for your child's success is that he/she introjects the American capitalist ethos."

---

[38] Ibid., 443.

Ravitch makes the point that the public school's purpose is "to teach children the general skills and knowledge that they need to succeed."[39] Even if the schools teach the values of a pluralist society (under attack by particularists) the criterion of success is measured against the way things are now. That is, the capitalist ethos and with it class divisions are simply not questioned. This system is defined as natural; minorities need only apply the "boot strap" strategy to become successful. The conclusion to this ideological syllogism is found in Ravitch's analysis of why certain minorities would choose a Particularist ethnocentric curriculum. She says:

> In school districts where most children are black and Hispanic, there has been a growing tendency to embrace particularism. Many of the children in these districts perform poorly in academic classes and leave school without graduating . . . Particularism is a *lure* [to these minority groups because] . . . it offers a less complicated anyodyne, one in which the children's academic deficiencies may be addressed—or set aside—by inflating their racial pride.[40]

Notice the quantifier in the sentence describing the minority children is "MANY," i.e., "Many of these children . . . perform poorly . . . leave school . . . have academic deficiencies." This description fits the category of children who are "at risk." Again, such an argument is political in two more senses.

First, the description deflects the issue of minority achievement away from the school and locates the deficiency within the individual child. Second, no mention of the children's social class, their "cultural capital," nor even the presence of discrimination are mentioned as possibilities that condition school success. The only category she uses to explain things is ethnic: these children are black or Hispanic. The implication is that such children are members of racial/ethnic groups which themselves are out of sync with the "true American culture." In this regard, black and Hispanic minorities demonstrate a deficiency. Ravitch concludes that an emphasis on a particularist curriculum reinforces these cultural differences and condemns these minority children to failure in the school and workplace. This argument at once disenfranchises working-class black and Hispanic minorities from power on educational grounds and covers over a systematic class bias.

---

[39] Ibid., 441.
[40] Ibid., 446.

If cultural hegemony is the principle operating Ravitch's cultural pluralism, then Schlesinger's text is the intellectual organ of that political ideology. His *The Disuniting of America* is a compelling text; two reasons why, seem obvious: first, Schlesinger opposes the politicized rhetoric of multiculturalism against a concern for preservation of the union. Second, his narrative appears as a disinterested example of historical analysis. In a word, Schlesinger appears to have overcome special pleading extremist ideologies and presented a larger truth. Ironically, the text's central message is chauvinistic: whatever one's skin color, ethnic ancestry, mother tongue, religion, or class position, one's ultimate identity is that of an American citizen.

Keeping in mind that my reading of the text searches for an answer to the question, "How does Schlesinger represent minority American culture?" what follows sets down the categories that are central to answering that question. Those categories include the American Creed, the ideological uses of history, and the Afrocentric and cultural pluralism paradigms.

Schlesinger argues that the American Creed is the source of our tradition as citizens. Moreover, it is an ethos that works as an instrument of socialization and a way of viewing the world:

> The American Creed had its antecedents, and these antecedents lay primarily in a British inheritance as recast by a century and a half of colonial experience. This . . . White Anglo-Saxon Protestant tradition was for two centuries . . . the dominant influence on American culture and society. This tradition provided the standard to which other immigrant nationalities were expected to conform, the matrix into which they would be assimilated."[41]

A quote from George Washington, himself, introduces Schlesinger's "Melting Pot" theory of cultural pluralism: "'Let them settle as individuals, prepared for intermixture with our people.' Then they would be assimilated to our customs, measures and laws: in a word, soon become one people. [An Emerson quote is more explicit:] 'America, this asylum of all nations and all European tribes—of the Africans and Polynesians will construct a new race . . . as vigorous as the New Europe which came out of the smelting pot of the Dark Ages.'"[42]

The ethical imperative of the American Creed which Americans "of

---

[41]   Arthur M. Schlesinger, Jr, *The Disuniting of America* (New York: W.W. Norton & Company, Inc. 1992), 27–28.

[42]   Ibid., 24, 27.

all national origins, religions, creeds and colors ... hold in commons [is] the most explicitly expressed system of general ideas of the essential dignity and equality of all human beings, of inalienable rights to freedom, justice, and opportunity."[43] In the face of the history of oppression toward ethnic immigrants and of the enduring racism directed against Afro-Americans, Schlesinger allows that "The Creed" meant "even more to blacks than to Whites, since it was the great means of pleading their unfulfilled rights [and, he argues that] the Second World War gave the Creed a new bite."[44] That is, if a crucial rationale for fighting Nazism included the rejection of the "Master Race" theory, a-fortiori the United States had to get its own house in order regarding race relations at home.

In fact, Schlesinger says while "the war did not end American racism, at least it drove much racial bigotry underground." Indeed, the revitalized Creed is seen as the engine that overcame past injustice: "emboldened [by it], blacks organized for equal opportunities [setting into motion] the civil rights revolution."[45] It is this overarching demand for equality in an Anglocentric culture that provoked new expressions of ethnic identity by the now-long resident "new immigration" from Southern and Eastern Europe. The Creed then, as an ethical imperative, reminds us who we are as a people; Schlesinger quotes American President Franklin Delano Roosevelt: "Americanism is not, and never was, a matter of race and ancestry. A good American is one who is loyal to this country and to our creed of liberty and democracy."[46]

All of this is a prelude to the legitimation of Schlesinger's model of the assimilated minority in the appeal to Israel Zangwill's 1908 play, "The Melting Pot." Zangwill is described as an English writer of Russian-Jewish origins, and his play is the story of young Jew who marries a Christian girl. This is an epic paradigm case of America and the assimilation of foreigners who come to her shores: America "is God's crucible, the Great Melting Pot. Where all the races of Europe are melting and reforming . . . what a stirring . . . Celt and Latin, Slav and Teuton, Greek and Syrian—Black and yellow."[47]

Against this salvivific process of enculturation, how are these

---

43   Ibid., 39.
44   Ibid., 40.
45   Ibid., 37.
46   Ibid., 32.
47   Ibid., 28.

128

hyphenated Americans seen? How are they to see themselves? Schlesinger answers by first calling forth the "Turner Thesis," which describes nineteenth century immigrant frontiersmen as "Americanized, liberated, and fused into a mixed race." He avers that Anglos "often dislike the newcomers . . . with their uncouth presence [and] alien religions. [Indeed, the newer wave of immigrants], Italians, Poles, Hungarians, Czechs, Slovaks, Russians [and] Jews, settled in the cities where their bizarre customs, dress, languages . . . excited new misgivings." Predictably, the cities were to divide into ethnic "enclaves [that] served as staging areas before entry was made into the larger and riskier American Life."[48]

Unmeltable ethnics, however, did not and still do not get it. Schlesinger reminds us of the etymology of the word "ethnic"; "it originally meant 'heathen' or 'pagan' . . . and had acquired an association with foreignness [but] since the 1960s, it definitely means non-Anglo minorities—a reversion to the original sense of being beyond the pale."[49] The text continues that since the sixties, "a cult of ethnicity" has developed, championed by "self-appointed spokesmen" who railed against the Anglocentric melting pot theory because it denies ethnics "role models" in the jargon—from their own ethnic ancestries."[50] The upshot is the codification into law of the 1974 Ethnic Heritage Studies Program Act—a statute Schlesinger says "compromised the historic right of Americans to decide their ethnic identity for themselves."[51]

Closely joined to the issue of identity is Schlesinger's description of history as a discipline, its proper use, and a criticism of those pseudo-historians whose work ferments political division within the United States. He argues that the discipline of history operates on our collective unconsciousness, as memory does for the individual psyche: "it is a means of defining national identity, [and] of shaping history itself." Properly, history is an instrument of disinterested intellectual inquiry "and of democracy" itself.[52]

Against this standard of "proper" history, the perversions of exculpatory history and its converse, compensatory history are exposed. The discussion ends with a surprising connecting myth and history.

---

48 Ibid., 41.
49 Ibid., 15.
50 Ibid., 43.
51 Ibid., 99.
52 Ibid., 53.

According to the text, all perversions of history share the same ideological task, namely to proselytize a nationalistic sense. On one hand, exculpatory history, works to justify the ruling class. Schlesinger allows that "American history [has been] long written in the interests of WASPS . . . and falsified by [the] suppression of uglier aspects of Anglo-callous discrimination against later immigrants [and] brutal racism against on-White minorities." He insists, however, there is a factual truth here; that "for almost all of this nation's history, the major decisions have been made by White Christian men."[53]

Compensatory history, on the other hand, is a divisive political weapon without concern for preserving the union. Especially in the hands of militant ideologues, this brand of history is actually a campaign of correction that seeps into the public school. He argues that the intent of such history is to allow the minority group to overcome the hegemonic Anglocentric culture; such a history is pseudo-history that is neither factual nor disinterested. This is a history as "social and psychological therapy [and is meant] to raise the minority group's self-esteem."[54] Since theirs is a history of being oppressed in America, Afro-Americans are targets of a virulent compensatory nationalism that emphasizes difference and separation from the society. Special attention on this score is directed toward the public school. One critic cited, Maulana Karenga, argues that:

> White education . . . cuts out Blacks, the fathers and mothers of mankind and human civilization, and [it] aims to turn Black students into obscene caricatures of Europe, pathetic imitators of their oppressors.[55]

Another Afrocentrist argues that public school inhibits the achievement of Afro-American children because it does not recognize the reality of

> Several distinct intelligences, of which the communication and calculation valued by Whites constitute only two. Other kinds of "intelligence" are singing and dancing, in both of which Blacks excel.[56]

Schlesinger next locates the pedagogy of compensatory history. He

---

[53]   Ibid., 49.
[54]   Ibid., 62.
[55]   Ibid., 63.
[56]   Ibid., 69.

pays special attention to Asa Hilliard's *Afro-American Baseline Essays.*
The latter were introduced into the Portland, Oregon public schools in
1987. Following the Baseline Guide, a revised history would teach
children the following:

> Egypt was a Black African country and the real source of the science and
> philosophy Western historians attribute to Greece. Africans . . . also invented
> birth control and carbon steel. They brought science, medicine, and the arts to
> Europe. Indeed, many European artists, such as Browning and Beethoven, were
> in fact "Afro-European." They . . . discovered America long before Columbus,
> and the original name of the Atlantic Ocean was the Ethiopian Ocean.[57]

A rebuttal of each of these claims is detailed in the next section of
the text: The Battle of the Schools. Even here, Schlesinger is
unambiguous: compensatory history is a tissue of lies and fabrications
and such history tribalizes America, setting citizen against citizen.

At the end of this discussion, Schlesinger repeats the theme that the
"purpose of history is not the presentation of self nor the indication of
identity, but the recognition of complexity and the search for
knowledge."[58] In the beginning of the chapter and almost as an aside,
Schlesinger makes some rather curious statements about the relationship
of history to nationalism, the mythic character of such history and the
purity of the discipline itself. He says that the use of history as a
mechanism of nationalism is a corruption. Moreover, such use was
"developed by intellectuals in the interests of aspiring elites." As if
mimicking Levi-Strauss' definition of myth, he adds, this kind of history
continues "to give individual lives meaning in an increasingly baffling
universe." Most surprising is this conclusion: "there is no such thing as a
pure history anyway."

I shall return to this later as an instance of what Derrida calls the
supplement. Here, I want to finish my description of the text to the last of
my categories: the couplet cultural pluralism and Afrocentricity.

Schlesinger's definition of the kind of history to be taught is actually
a moral pronouncement. Good history "promotes an understanding of the
world and the past. Good history expresses then a pluralistic approach,
while also preserving the ideas of an overarching American nationality."
Bad history is false: it has a fundamental political purpose, namely to
help ethical/racial minorities overcome a sense of inferiority. Bad history

---

[57]   Ibid., 99.
[58]   Ibid., 55.

is the "cult of ethnicity [which] exaggerates differences, intensifies resentments and . . .drives . . . wedges between races and nationalities."[59]

Not much space is given to exposing cultural pluralist historiography. Instead, Schlesinger criticizes historians of bad history and their work. His method is to set down an example of bad history and then refute its claims by appealing to a good historian, i.e., one who supports Schlesinger's criticisms. One further feature, especially when dealing with the bad history of Afrocentrism and the Baseline Essays, Schlesinger quotes celebrated Afro-Americans whose words appear to contradict Afrocentrism. Specifically, Schlesinger examines Afrocentric claims about the racial composition of ancient Egypt, the connections of Black Egypt to ancient Western philosophy, and a Baseline story regarding an Afro-American scientific hero.

Afrocentrist history teaches that ancient Egypt was essentially a black African country—the foundation of ancient Greece's intellectual legacy. The source of this claim is attributed to Martin Bernal's *Black Athena*. Among the counterfactual, that Schlesinger offers is the testimony of the Egyptologist, Frank J. Yurco, who argues that there were gradations of color in the ancient Egyptians, ranging from a light Mediterranean type to that of the darker Nubians. Nonetheless, he adds that ancient Egyptians would find the issue of race "meaningless" and the assignment of racial labels "primitive."[60]

Miriam Lictheim, another Egyptologist, is categorical: "The Egyptians were not Nubians, and the original Nubians were not Black." Nubia gradually became black because black people migrated northward out of Central Africa. Still another expert says that claims about a Black Egypt are "an attempt by American blacks to provide themselves with an ancient history linked to that of the high civilization of ancient Egypt. Evidence is that it was a mixed Mediterranean people."[61]

A further development of the Black Egypt myth is that such headliners of Western civilization as Aristotle and Pythagoras stole their ideas from Black Egyptian scholars. Regarding the Pythagoras claim, an expert claims that although the Egyptians knew of Pythagorean relationships, "the theorem [or] proof of the relationships were Hellenic."[62]

---

[59]   Ibid.,15.
[60]   Ibid.,77.
[61]   Ibid.
[62]   Ibid.

The argument that Aristotle stole his ideas is tied to the story that Alexander the Great pillaged the library of Alexandria on the *Stagirite's* behalf. Schlesinger's counterfactual is that the library of Alexandria "was not established until half a century after Alexander and Aristotle died."[63] The clear implication in the text is that such fabrications are the warp and woof of the Afrocentric ideological cloth.

The text produces the Baseline Essay of the Charles R. Drew story as an archetype of bad history. Drew was the Afro-American scientist who devised the method to preserve blood plasma. According to the Baseline Essay, a critically injured Drew died because several nearby white hospitals would not provide a blood transfusion. In rebuttal, the "black scholar, Rayford Logan, [says] conflicting versions to the contrary, Drew received prompt medical attention."[64]

The next attack on Afrocentrism takes the form of a *reductio ad absurdum*. Put as questions, Schlesinger asks: What are the implications of arguing that the black mind works differently? How can Afrocentrists point to a pantheon of Afro-American greats when they later deny Africa first? What positive results derive from the Afrocentrist attempt to enculturate Afro-American children into African traditions? "Should public education . . . perpetuate separate ethnic and racial subcultures?" The answer to each question seems to turn the Afrocentrist's ideology on its head by revealing the absurd logic of its conclusions.

Schlesinger quotes the black psychologist Wade Nobles on the difference between the working of black and white minds. Nobles is quoted as saying: "this difference stems from basic African philosophy, which dictates the values, customs, attitudes, and behavior of Africans in Africa and the New World." Schlesinger claims this argument is a form of biological determinism, i.e., "race determines mentality [Schlesinger argues this is] another word for racism."[65]

Indeed, according to Schlesinger, the connections that Afrocentrists make to an African homeland and African culture are not only recent, they are denied by major historical Afro-American figures, who themselves espoused the Western tradition and championed the preeminence of America, not Africa. For example, Frederick Douglass is quoted: "Not to say one idea has given rise to more oppression . . . toward the colored people of this country . . . than that which makes

---

63   Ibid., p. 79

64   Ibid., p. 80.

65   Ibid., p. 82.

Africa, not America, their home." W.E.B. DuBois is cited: "the complete absorption of Western modes . . . [was] imperative if we were to survive all; in brief, there is nothing so indigenous, so completely, 'made in America' as we."[66]

Along this line, Schlesinger has the same cultural heroes traced to their intellectual roots in Dead White Men. Frederick Douglass on the book, *The Columbian Orator* (a book that contained speeches by Burke and Sheridan, among others): "What I got from Sheridan was a bold denunciation of slavery." From W.E.B. Dubois: "I sit with Shakespeare . . . across the color line I move in arm with Balzac and Dumas." The testimony of Ralph Ellison: "I read Marx, Freud, T.S. Eliot, Pound, Gertrude Stein and Hemingway. Books which seldom, if ever, mentioned Negroes were to release me from whatever segregated idea I might have had in my human possibilities."[67]

Given this evidence, what point is there in the Afrocentrist enculturation of the curriculum? None. The text quotes prominent black scholars who reject Afrocentrism as an impediment. William Raspberry states that Afrocentric education will make black children "less competent in the culture in which they have to compete." Orlando Paterson calls the black historian's attempt to get the black man into the birth of civilization story, "the three P's approach: Black history as princes, pyramids and pageantry." Henry Louis Gates says: "Afrocentrists . . . are advocates not of Cultural Pluralism but of black ethnocentrism."[68]

The obvious conclusion to all of the above is that the school should not perpetuate separate subcultures and that when religious or ethnic pressure groups attempt to "approve or veto anything that is taught in public schools, the fatal line is crossed between Cultural Pluralism and ethnocentrism. [What is lost] is the old idea that whatever our ethnic base, we are all Americans together."[69]

My reading of Schlesinger will return to his objection that Afrocentrism is bad history. It will look again at the historical context of the quotes he uses. I shall argue that Schlesinger's argument is curiously an ahistorical, political message intended to promote American nationalism. The effect is that the Afro-American culture as a

---

[66] Ibid., 83.
[67] Ibid., 91.
[68] Ibid., 95.
[69] Ibid., 136.

supplement is reinforced. To prove this assertion I shall first turn to Derrida's use of the term "supplement."

My use of Derrida's construct does not repeat any of his specific analyses. Instead, I will show the kind of moves a reader employs when his/her reading is informed by the supplement. Put differently, I am first interested in showing how the supplement works. Having done that, the supplement will be applied to the categories previously culled from the Schlesinger text.

Taken in its usual sense, a supplement is something added that supplies a deficiency for what is lacking. Derrida builds on this usage and refashions the supplement over into a tool to deconstruct texts.

Following the structuralist discovery that acts of signification depend on *différance,* Derrida pulls out the binary oppositions within a text, first locating the term that is primary, i.e., that term which is the ground, the *eidos,* or key word of the text. It is this term that establishes the hierarchical system that runs throughout the chain of significations within the text. For example, a key set of oppositions in the text is that of American/ethnic. Obviously, the essential term in the couplet is American, the accidental or marginal term in the text is ethnic. Derrida argues that the second term should be treated as a negative version of the first, i.e., in my example, ethnic is the supplement to American. But what is crucial regarding any supplement is that the supplement not only is the hidden device that fills a lack in the primary term, also the supplement is that feature in the text that overturns authoritative interpretations. Moreover, the supplement appears marginal because it often resides in unverified terms or premises that actually ground the text. Or, the supplement may even appear as an aside within the text, i.e., as a footnote. But the supplement, like a railway switch, brings together opposing lines of the argument and the supplement works to subvert these oppositions, overcoming the hierarchy within the text.

Overcoming the hierarchy of the text means reading in a new way. It means disrupting and replacing the privileged voice of the text that channels our ordinary received reading of the text. In a new critical reading, the supplement emerges not as inessential, foreign or added on, but as the necessary part of the signifying chain that fills the lack within the essential term. The result is that the text is reinscribed.

The above is crucial once the text is framed politically as an ideological discourse. Following Terry Eagleton, I use the term ideology to mean a legitimatising horizon that enables and accommodates certain kinds of 'meanings' and value production [moreover it is an a priori] kind of moral, political, and categorical imperative. Practically then, the distinctions between "is" and "ought," as well as the separation between the ethical, the political, and the theoretical are wiped out.

Keeping the constructs of the supplement and ideology in mind, I shall now turn to the first category, the American Creed. As previously seen, the American Creed is presented as the ethos of American society, the instrument of socialization and the definition of the good. The creed, for Schlesinger, as it was for Ravitch, becomes a form of cultural hegemony: sociopolitical and historical questions are reduced to politically neutral abstract questions of culture. In this mystification, the real power relations within culture are hidden. Again, the creed in this text depoliticizes the social construction of reality by appealing to a definition of culture that has been identified as Universalist Humanism. This is a representation found in cultural products and texts, which delivers so-called timeless and universal values that span history and point to a cultural ideal. This representation is the fullness of an ethical model of the human, i.e., a universal human essence that transcends political differences, depicts developmental stages of becoming human, defines human freedom and authenticity, and is a model that the minority disenfranchised are to mirror in order to become empowered.

The Swedish sociologist Gunnar Myrdal coined the notion of an American Creed more than fifty years ago. Simply put, the Creed recapitulates the phrase from the *Declaration of Independence,* that "all men are created equal," i.e., a creed of equality and liberty for all. Put in historical context, the Creed is the moral exemplar that propels Myrdal's analysis of rin the 1940s. For Myrdal, the Creed elicited a moral unease in the dominant white majority regarding race relations: The Creed exposed a lack in the dominant group. Schlesinger, however, decontextualizes the Creed by transforming it into a Universalist Humanistic principle that has guided the country from the beginning. In this guise, the Creed becomes a fetish, a metaphysical trans-historical principle that papers over real political race and class antagonisms. Schlesinger does this by coupling the Creed to a nationalistic ideology of Melting Pot theory. Using this technique, ethnics and Afro-Americans are shown why their ancestors were, and they themselves must be, reborn as Anglicized Americans—a process that is found to be lacking, especially in Afro-Americans today. The Creed, therefore, represents a monocultural society as an ideal. Politically, it perpetuates the status quo by casting those who would resist it as un-American.

Under the Creed, ethnics are provided an ideal of freedom, justice, and opportunity. Further, a pantheon of American heroes are called on to extol the monocultural ideal of assimilating all to an Anglocentric America. The tone is quasi-theological: immigrants are in a state of incompletion, i.e., immigrants are not fully American until they have undergone the process of assimilation. This means they must renounce their ethnic allegiances. With this "purification," they are born again as Americans.

The Melting Pot is the hidden political apriori that frames the Creed and is repeated by Schlesinger's world historical figures. In Schlesinger's words, the American Creed represents "the White Anglo-Saxon Protestant tradition." This is the standard to which other immigrant nationalities were expected to conform, the matrix into which they would be assimilated. George Washington is quoted as saying, "immigrants are *prepared* for intermixture . . . assimilated . . . soon become one people."[70] Emerson emphasizes "America [as] this *asylum* of all nations and the energy of all European tribes of the Africans and the Polynesians will construct a new race."[71] There are two messages here. The first is that America is a refuge for people who are in a state of privation or lack. And the notion of a "new race" sets down the fiction that racial amalgamation will easily and swiftly occur. In this sense, immigrants are the supplement to Anglo-American. The assimilated immigrant is on the way toward overcoming differences. The amalgamated immigrants then realize that children will have the potential of becoming a part of the universalized American essence.

However, the problem of racial amalgamation has not been resolved in America. Skin color remains an essential marker of discrimination and economic class. Obviously, Africans were not immigrants—they were chattel; even the framers of the American Constitution tactfully accepted that.

The Creed not only legitimizes the Anglocentric culture, it becomes a metaphysical entity turning the historical-political world upside down. For Schlesinger, the Creed becomes a source of the civil rights revolution. He says, "emboldened by it, blacks organized for equal

---

[70] Ibid., 25.
[71] Ibid., 24.

opportunities. Even ethnics moved by the Creed [were] provoked [into] new expressions of ethnic identity."[72]

With these asides, Schlesinger reverts to the most important function of the Creed, namely assimilation. He chooses Zangwill's play, "The Melting Pot," as a model for the American experience: America is God's crucible, "where all races of Europe are melting and reforming."[73] Even the historian Frederick Jackson Turner's thesis that a unique American character was forged by the independent frontier men moving West gets into the picture: these people were "Americanized, liberated and fused into a mixed race."[74] Later, I shall show how Schlesinger intertwines the Melting Pot into the moral ideal; Schlesinger allows the stew has not always commingled. Again, immigrants were lacking, in a sense they were *not fully human*, the "newer immigrants displayed *bizarre* customs dress and languages."[75] Unprepared, and in a state of privation, these immigrants lived in "enclaves," *staging* areas where they were *prepared* for American life. Conveniently, no mention is made of institutionalized racism or of factory towns that are populated by an immigrant proletariat. Instead, Schlesinger next reinforces the idea that to be an ethnic originally denoted a nonbeliever, an idolater, or one who is beyond the confines of community. This is a nice fit against the metaphysical theological description of the Creed.

The moral point is obvious; those latter-day ethnics, who reject the Melting Pot, speak in tongues of a foreign religion, and their work is heresy. Such ethnics are divisive to the union. For example, their efforts brought about "The Ethnic Heritage Studies Program Act." As a result, Americans can no longer choose their ethnic identity themselves. What could this claim about ethnic identity mean? Historically, and by law, a person whose ancestry was one-sixteenth black was defined as a black. The infamous Jim Crow laws are illustrative. I use these examples not because they are obvious, but because they preview the way the text's arguments turn against themselves. For example, all of the above examples reveal ethnic as the marginal category subsumed by the Creed and its corollary American. The ethnic not only fills the lack in the Creed; ethnic defines that lack.

---

[72] Ibid., 41.
[73] Ibid., 32.
[74] Ibid.
[75] Ibid., 28.

The key word in Schlesinger's chapter on the ideological uses of history, is history itself. That is, he gives a definition of the discipline of history, the proper uses of history, and the connection of fact to historical interpretation. Contrasting against this definition of history are two corruptions or marginal cases: exculpatory history and compensatory history.

Schlesinger defines history as an instrument of disinterested intellectual inquiry; moreover, history is the recognition of complexity, the search for knowledge, and the recovery of fact.

What corruptions of this paradigm of history share is the presentation of history slanted, toward and meant to promote, a form of nationalism. The difference between the two, however, is polar. Exculpatory history attempts to legitimate the rule of the dominant classes over those who are powerless. Exculpatory history papers over and rationalizes the brutalization of the oppressed. The end of exculpatory history is the preservation of the political status quo. Schlesinger alludes to the fact that the WASP power structure in the past discriminated against non-white citizens and immigrant groups and then suppressed this truth in accounts of official history. However, he tempers this by saying that for most of our history, WASP men were in charge. That is, exculpatory American history presents *facts,* even if those facts are distorted to promote an allegiance to the ruling classes.

Schlesinger is far more interested in compensatory history and those pseudo-historians who purvey it. Pseudo-historians present a history that is neither disinterested nor factual. Indeed, compensatory history ultimately has the intent of separating disaffected groups from the union: building a separate nation and correcting the "so-called history" delivered by the ruling Anglocentric power structure. Obviously, compensatory history works on many levels; essentially, though, it is a fabrication directed to and by minorities as a means to enhance that minority group's self-esteem, even at the expense of telling the big lie.

Schlesinger looks especially at Afrocentrist ideology. He looks first at two rather typical claims: first, that the schools are the mouthpiece of the Anglo power structure that relegates Afro-American children into caricatures of their white oppressors. The second claim is that definitions of black intelligence as inferior are premised on the racist view of intelligence. Schlesinger is especially concerned about Hilliard's revisionist history, the Afro-American Baseline Essays. The latter is explicated in detail in the next chapter. Suffice it to say, Schlesinger will become a harsh critic of the Baseline Curriculum.

It appears, however, that the binary oppositions between pure history and its corruptions fall apart. Put differently, compensatory history and pure history are different sides of the same coin. If, as we have already seen in Schlesinger's own words, "there is no such thing as pure history anyway," and if pure history is a means of defining national identity, then at least two things follow. First, we cannot rehabilitate a pure history that never existed. Instead, we must examine the varieties of historiography in use, primary sources, and the categories that are applied to interpretation. The latter are transcendental in the sense that they set down the limits and conditions of historical investigation.

More than that, when Schlesinger argues that history is at the service of democracy and that it shapes our collective consciousness, he is arguing that history is in the service of nationalism.

Even more crucial is his aside that history "gives individual lives meaning in an increasingly battling universe."[76] This interpretation of history is Levi-Strauss' definition of myth. Facts may be a part of myth, but they are accidental, not essential. With this turn in the argument, the supplement compensatory history has been collapsed into its apparent opposite, disinterested history. The fullness of the supplementary nature of the Afrocentric paradigm is revealed in the next section.

The goals of the chapter "The Battle of the Schools" are plain. It first attacks the Afrocentrist historians and their work, and then demonstrates that an Afrocentric curriculum in the schools is a very negative subject to adopt. Schlesinger's technique is straightforward: he cites representative Afrocentric claims and then appeals to another expert to refute those claims. To reinforce the criticisms, the text inserts the words of Afro-American cultural heroes. Each figure cited repeats the same theme: Afro-Americans are not Africans; they are Americans. With remarkable redundancy, the point is made that Afrocentric history and Afrocentric school curriculum promote division and racial resentment. cultural pluralism is the truth we must embrace.

The keyword is cultural pluralism, while the opposition supplement is Afrocentrism. With some irony, Schlesinger ties the origin of the term "cultural pluralism" to a 1915 piece published in "The Nation," written by Horace Kallen and entitled "Democracy and the Melting Pot." Kallen's point was that whatever else men may change, they cannot

---

[76]   Ibid., 68.

change their ethnic origins. In Kallen's terms, neither the Jew nor the Pole can change his grandfather's identity. For Schlesinger, what matters is that Kallen prescribed cultural pluralism as a "democracy of nationalities cooperating voluntarily and autonomously . . . a multiplicity in a unity."[77] Cultural pluralism is the moral exemplar both of good history and the proper school curriculum. If such a curriculum is Eurocentric, one must remember American civilization has its origins in Europe. Moreover, Schlesinger argues that Europe is the source of origin for eighty percent of the American people. "Of course, the [other] twenty percent and their contributions should be integrated into the curriculum too, which is the point of Cultural Pluralism."[78]

On its surface, the model of cultural pluralism and its legacy appear reinforced by neutral facts. However, cultural pluralism is a political definition of the socioeconomic world, if only by omission. When Schlesinger accepts the Kallen definition of cultural pluralism he acknowledges that the latter was attacking Anglo-centered assimilationist views. The supplement, though, to this is found in the claim that such criticisms "would reasonably assume the solidity of the overarching framework" of racial/ethnic relations."[79] Indeed, the text makes the point that without this acceptance of an overarching frame (i.e., an Anglocentric capitalist society) there would be a "weakening of the original idea of a single society."[80]

As the central supplement to cultural pluralism, Afrocentricity is rebutted point by point. Previously, I alluded to the counterfactuals made by opposing experts. For instance, the Egyptologist, Yurco, is seen rejecting "The Black Athena" thesis, and a rebuttal is made of the claim that Aristotle and Pythagoras plagiarized Ancient Black Egyptians. What is curious here is that the falsity of Afrocentric claims is accepted *prima facie* on the basis of the credibility of opposing experts.

Setting aside this objection, presume that each of the expert rebuttals is true. What the Afrocentrist has left are simply the words of Afro-American cultural heroes. None, according to Schlesinger, sought to affirm an African identity; each was an American first. The text quotes both Frederick Douglass, who rejected the view that American blacks saw Africa as their home, and DuBois, who argued that blacks were so

---

[77] Ibid., 36.
[78] Ibid., 122.
[79] Ibid., 37.
[80] Ibid., 43.

completely assimilated that they were "indigenous" to America. We are reminded, though, that the words these men set down were in English. The source of these ideas were those of white Europeans. DuBois found inspiration from Shakespeare and Balzac; Ellison was schooled in Marx, Freud, Eliot, and Pound.

Now, in one sense, the problem of responding to such vows of allegiance, especially the issue of whether Africa or America is the real homeland of Afro-Americans, is rather easy to resolve. The second set of quotes, though, appears to prove the dependence of Afro-American cultural heroes, and by implication the Afro-American culture, on the Anglocentric culture.

Looking first at the homeland issue, what can be said is that both Douglass and DuBois were arguing that blacks must be recognized as full citizens of the United States. Douglass' remarks were made in the context of the adoption of the Fourteenth Amendment to the American Constitution. For example, previously, the Constitution made a compromise in which five slaves were equivalent to three whites. DuBois similarly was arguing that blacks must be accorded the protections of the law granted to all citizens.

Schlesinger then has taken the political meaning of these quotes out of their historical context to serve his ideological purpose. Put differently, DuBois and Douglass, though writing at different times, wanted to reinforce the rights and the legal protections of Afro-Americans as citizens of the United States.

When Schlesinger reminds us that Douglass wrote in the English language, or that DuBois and Ellison are praising Shakespeare, Balzac, Marx, and Eliot, the argument takes on a new political conclusion. That is, giants like Ellison, DuBois, and Douglass were dependent on original ideas taken from the repository of Western civilization, i.e., the ideas of dead white men. Even more, the mother tongue of Ellison and DuBois is the English language. One does not have to have familiarity with the Sapir-Whorf theory to understand that language is the critical determinant of culture.

The conclusion is plain, then: Afro-American culture, even in the best light, must be viewed as secondary and lacking—indeed, as a supplementary culture. This is a charitable reading of Schlesinger, though. Stripped of history and myth, denied cultural heroes, and with reduced Black English to Standard English, the Afro-American culture is erased. In Eliot's terms, Afro-Americans are "hollow men." Better yet, following Ellison, the Afro-American culture is invisible.

Such a picture represents the triumph of Anglo-ethnocentrism. This is the cultural pluralist Melting Pot ideology. This is an epistemic principle that is at once ahistorical and hegemonic in its legitimation of the socioeconomic status quo.

Using Derrida's construct of the *supplement,* I have read Arthur Schlesinger and the Ravitch texts as ideologies seen fundamentally as a criticism of minority political interests. Specifically, by using the text's categories of the American Creed, History, and the Cultural Pluralist— Afrocentric paradigms, the immigrant Southern and Eastern European cultures, and most especially the Afro-American culture were seen as supplements to the dominant Anglocentric culture.

The fullness of the supplement, though, as a critical tool, revealed how the cultural pluralist argument turns against itself. Certain key constructs were set against apparently marginal oppositions. What was revealed is that *The Disuniting of America* attacks on minority culture, and particularly Afro nation-building, masks what is itself a nationalistic polemic that demands minorities form a more perfect union by identification with the dominant culture.

The application of Derrida's techniques of deconstruction: the *supplement* and *grafting* continues the critical conversation between phenomenology and structuralist thought. *Derrida's emphasis on the priority of the written over the spoken word* has crucial significance in the break up of Husserl's description of time-consciousness. That is, from Saussure, the play of difference is radicalized and the stability of myths that encode subjectivity are subject to deconstruction. Chapter Eight extends the critical conversation to Lacan's Freudian model. The theme is Luce Irigaray's excavation of the political domination of women in the phallocentric culture, where women are seen as subjects without a voice.

Chapter 8
Irigaray: Reading Sexual Différance

The political ideology of male dominance is so embedded in our collective consciousness that it works as a silent epistemic principle, organizing our experience of the world but passing unnoticed. And, historically the American public school is an apparatus out of which this invisible ideology of sexual discrimination is legitimated: Sadker and Sadker's study of public school textbooks shows a profound contrast in the portrayal of males and females. Males are described as competitive, creative, autonomous power users who avoid anything feminine. But females exhibit dependence, passivity, incompetence, and a concern about appearance and domesticity.[1]

Carol Gilligan has excavated the ideology of male superiority in the work of Erickson, Freud, Kohlberg, and Piaget.[2] Indeed, Jane Roland Martin has argued that academic disciplines have excluded women from the subject matter and distorted their image according to "the male image

---

[1]   Mura Sadker and David Sadker, "Sexism in the Classroom: From Grade School to Graduate School." In Justice, Ideology, and Education, eds. Edward Stevens, Jr. & George Wood (McGraw-Hill, 1995), 109.

[2]   Carol Gilligan, In a Different Voice (Cambridge: Harvard University Press, 1982), 7

of [women] and denied the feminine by forcing women into a masculine world."[3] The conclusion: to be born a male means to acquire normative subjectivity. For example, so-called gender "personality traits" now assume an ontological status: the male is the normative subject and is characterized as active, rational, and competitive. By contrast, the female is construed as a lesser version of the male and she is characterized as passive, emotional, and nurturing.[4]

This chapter exposes the mechanisms of male hegemony, or what has more specifically been labeled phallocentrism, by appealing to the constructs of the psychoanalyst/philosopher Luce Irigaray. Her critical model is important on several counts: it deconstructs sexist stereotypes about women, turning these distortions against themselves and reclaiming gender difference; it provides correctives to our understanding of psychosexual development; and it gives new direction to the teaching of ethical decision-making and provides a dialogical model for the sexes.

My exposition begins with a definition of ideology set in the context of the structuralism idiom. This linguistic reading emphasizes the formation of gendered subjectivity at its ground zero in the drama of the Oedipus Complex. Specifically, I begin with Irigaray's revisionist reading of the Freudian structuralist Jacques Lacan. Special attention is paid to Irigaray's political descriptions of the phallus and female genitalia. Finally, connections are made to her postfeminist model of ethical reasoning and the construction of a new dialogical feminine subjectivity.

Following Terry Eagleton, I use the term "ideology" to mean those cultural discourses that "ratify and legitimate oppressive political systems [using] devices of unification, universalization and rationalization. [At the level of lived experience,] ideology gives individuals values and beliefs relevant to social tasks and to the reproduction of the social order."[5] In semiotic terms, this is a false representation. Specifically, the signified referent "women" is presented as an unchanging and deficient human who unknowningly internalizes the political interests of the oppressor that are in play, but hidden. Put

---

[3]   Jane Roland Martin, "Excluding Women From the Educational Realm," *Harvard Educational Review,* 52, no. 2 (May 1982), 133.

[4]   Several critics are explicit on this score. Cf. Carol G. Gilligan, *In A Different Voice,* (Cambridge: Harvard University Press, 1982), 7.

[5]   C.f. Terry Eagleton, *Ideology* (New York: Verso, 1991).

simply, the signifiers of this representation do double duty; not only do they mediate and interpret reality for the subject, the subject himself/herself is an active participant sustains this representation of the world. What results is a politics of exclusion, which fixes a unified identity for the male and simultaneously declares the female to be a void.

Luce Irigaray is a revisionist Freudian/philosopher whose political agenda is to reinstate the ontological difference between the genders. She is not properly a feminist: she rejects the demand for women's equality with men; she inscribes difference between the sexes by discussing the female pudenda, i.e., the labia or the lips which do not speak; she dismisses the disembodied male epistemology of neutral, rational objectivity, privileging instead embodied emotions as necessary in ethical reasoning; she couches her work in female mimicry; and in all these things she seems to be what even her feminist critics attack—an essentialist who reinforces male sexist stereotypes of women. With this preview I turn now to gloss Irigaray's attack on Lacan, whose work she views as a postmodern ideological expression of male hegemony.

Jacques Lacan was a crucial influence, one-time mentor, and colleague in Irigaray's training as a structuralist Freudian. Her mimicry of Lacan is evident as she at once adopts and criticizes his categories. She locates his phallocentrism in Lacan's description of the process of the Oedipal Conflict in which the child acquires language and is initiated into the Symbolic Order of Culture. To recapitulate, the Symbolic Order represents all of the institutions of society. And with the acquisition of language, the child becomes a full participant in the Symbolic Order: she/he takes on an identity, gains recognition, and is positioned as a gendered member of society. But Irigaray's analysis exposes the Oedipus mechanism as the site of a woman's oppression.

Her critique exposes the primacy Lacan imputes to the possession of the penis. Having a penis previews a different political agenda for boys. Implicitly acknowledging that, Lacan argues that he is dealing with a reading of psychosexual development and culture; he simply presents the phallus as the prime signifier. That is, Lacan argues that culture translates the physical penis into the symbolic phallus.[6] But Irigaray insists, despite his protestation, that the cultural symbol of the phallus bears the trace of the physical penis. Put differently, in the margins of Lacan's apparatus, the phallus legislates the male's psychological

---

[6]   C.f. Jacques Lacan, *Ecrits*, trans. Alan Sheridan (New York: W.W. Norton & Company, Inc. 1977).

146

milestones as natural and universal. Female development is treated as a variation of the male. But this is a variation of sameness, which is inferior, deficient, and lacking. Physically and symbolically, women lack the male member and appear instead as a hole.

To get hold of the Lacanian position and Irigaray's critique, I will now briefly review pivotal episodes in Lacan's reading of the formation of subjectivity, the *Mirror Phase* and the *fort-da game,* pointing to the culmination of both in the language of the unconscious.

The Mirror Phase describes the male infant in front of a mirror who is enthralled by the image of his autonomous body standing erect and moving at will. This mirror image is an illusion, in which the child misrecognizes himself. So absolute is this misrecognition in the child's consciousness that the physical presence of the adult holding him upright is pushed aside.

The child believes: "I felt myself immediately to be, I am the image of myself offered by the mirror, an ideal fictitious imaginary me which the specular image is outline." [7] And, through this glass darkly, the child grasps his separation from the mother.

The second Lacanian reading is of the previously discussed *fort/da* game.[8] This is Freud's psychoanalytical account of his grandson playing with a cotton reel, rhythmically bringing into or lowering out of sight an object attached to the string. In linguistic terms, the object stands for/is the signifier of the present or absent mother, which the child now symbolically controls.

For Lacan, later in the Symbolic phase of development the child must renounce and repress possession of the mother because of the symbolic fear of castration. Crucially, the boy's desire for the mother represents a nostalgic return to a natural unmediated, prediscursive state in the womb. But remember, Lacan says the boy's identification with the father is mediated by language. Ultimately, the boy's maturation demands that he assume his split subjectivity. Subjectivity is split, in the sense that the child must give up oneness with the mother and be subject to never-ending desire in the search for substitute symbolic satisfaction, which language initiates, and which is exposed in the *fort/da* game. Lacan's description of a boy counting himself with his brothers is

7   Jacques Lacan, "Le Stade due Miroir comme formateur dufonction due je," Revue Francaise de Psychanalyse 13 no. 4 (October December 1949): 449-455

8   Luce Irigary, *This Sex Which Is Not One,* trans. Catherine Porter (Ithaca: Cornell University Press, 1985), 34–67.

another example. As the boy counts, "Paul, Earnest, and me," his very act of counting demands a repression of his direct unmediated bodily self. This is similar to the self inseparable from, and identified with, the immediacy of the natural mother.[9] But in counting, the boy moves to the linguistic field and identifies with the independent symbolic self, subject to "the Law of the Father." It is the boy who counts in the Symbolic Order. This episode repeats the mirror phase, this time the specular self and language are bound together in the misrecognition of a personal unified autonomous subject.

And, with movement to the cultural realm, the boy accepts the promised satisfaction of other women in his future. Through language then, the boy deflects original desire. As he ratifies the "Name of the Father/Symbolic Order," he becomes a participant.

To summarize, for Lacan, discursive practices construct subjectivity. In the Oedipal drama, the female/mother is identified with the natural, lower, prediscursive material state; the male/father is identified with the higher discursive symbolic state. The themes of separation, threatened violence, and mastery are central to this metaphorical description. But the dominant theme is specular. Sight, more specifically the gaze, directs the *fort/da* game, the misrecognition of the mirror phase, and, most especially, the male child's corporeal awareness of the penis. The scopic regime of the gaze is the transcendental ground of male sexuality, identity, and truth. Irigaray's response to this is a critique meant to "jam the phallocentric machinery."

She begins with a close reading of Freud's description of female sexuality in its relationship to the male; she says: "A single genital apparatus—the male organ [becomes a transcendental signifier] fundamental for the 'infantile sexual organization of both sexes.'"[10] To call the male organ the transcendental signifier is to claim that in its discursive or symbolic form as the phallus, the male organ is the marker, origin, or presence that sets down the limits and conditions of gender politics in the culture. Put simply, the castration complex shows female lack and passivity; simultaneously, it ensconces male power and dominion. For example, with a glimpse of the female genitalia, the boy recoils in horror at the spectacle "of nothing to see." But this sight reinforces the threat of his own castration. The girl conversely understands castration not as a threat but as a *fait accompli*. "Compared

[9]   Lacan, *Ecrits*, 103–104.
[10] Irigaray, 35.

to the boy she has no sex, or at least what she thought was a valuable sex organ (the clitoris) is only a truncated penis." Indeed, her lot is that of "'lack,' 'atrophy' (of the sexual organ) and 'penis envy'; the penis being the only sexual organ of recognized value."[11] But for Freud, penis envy and his stress on the importance of the clitoral erogenous zone is changed with the girl's maturity: she shifts erogenous zones from the clitoris to the vagina, which, according to Freud, "is now valued as the place of shelter for the penis; it enters into the heritage of the womb. For Freud, most importantly, this entails and legitimates a "move toward passivity that is absolutely indispensable to the advent of femininity."[12]

Summarizing the above reveals the Freudian/Lacanian model as phallocentric ideology. Each of the elements of ideology: nature, universalism, rationalization, unity, and the power both to position and silence the female other are present. The Oedipus Complex is described as a natural actuation of human potentials that occur universally (crossculturally): the process explains how a child develops psychosexually; how that process is bound up with language; and most importantly, why the man is "naturally" more dominant, while women are passive. In this rationalization, the political conclusion is that a woman has a subordinate position without a voice.

Lacan's paradigm is the male meta-narrative, in which the phallus is the transcendental signifier or presence. A woman by contrast is an absence.

Later, I will return to the phallus as transcendental signifier, man as presence and women as absence, in Irigaray's deconstruction of Lacan's arguments. Before getting into the specifics of Irigaray's deconstruction of Freud/Lacan, I want to flesh out the issues that motivate her controversial method of criticism. Several questions emerge: How can phallocentrism be disrupted? What is the connection of phallocentrism to philosophy? Why not seek equality with men? What does it mean to say that a woman does not exist?

Disrupting phallocentrism begins with the recognition that female sexuality is constructed within male parameters. Remembering that phallocentrism is specular and that female lack is based on the economy of the same (that is the male), the task is to reopen the discourse that constructs gender. Irigaray says that the point is to pry out of them [males] what they have borrowed that is feminine, from the feminine to

---

[11] Ibid., 50.
[12] Ibid., 52.

make them "render up [and] give back what they owe, for example the sceneography that makes representation."[13] She argues the philosophical logos is the source of "the power to reduce all others to the economy of the same."[14] Philosophy is the hidden mirror that allows the logos, the subject, to reduplicate itself, to reflect itself by itself. Most important, philosophical discourses are essentially political and "no matter how mediate they may be, are none the less politically determined."[15] Put simply, women are in the position of exclusion: "Their exclusion is internal to an order from which nothing escapes."[16] The conclusion of this is captured in Irigaray's quote from Lacan: "There is no woman who is not excluded by the nature of words . . . they [i.e., women] don't know what they are saying [when they complain] and that's the whole difference between them and me."[17]

Having said that, is there any leverage left to a woman? Irigaray says, "yes." Women may not exist according to this linguistic order, but she "threatens as a sort of prediscursive reality to disrupt its order."[18] And this is the point of Irigaray's refusal to seek equality, which would be under the "Law of the Father." Better to attack the presence of the transcendental signifier, the phallus, in order to reclaim a woman's existence.

Naming the phallus as a transcendental signifier is to call it a metaphysical entity. Overcoming its political dominion requires a deconstruction to overcome the ahistorical pretense of presence, which results when content and representation are conflated. That is, the difference between the signified reality and the signified concept is erased. Recovering difference (in Derrida's terms, *différance*) demands the rupture of the self-identity of signifier and signified.

The phallus is a case in point in which *différance* is suppressed. It is one instance of "the lived reduction of the opacity of the signifier and signified, the origin of what [is called] presence."[19] Contrary to the phallus, metaphysical claim to ground, origin, and presence, *différance,* it

---

13   Ibid., 75.

14   Ibid., 11.

15   Ibid., 12.

16   Ibid., 87–88.

17   Jacques Lacan, "Encore, Le Seminare XX," in *This Sex Which Is Note One*, (Paris 1975), 87.

18   Ibid., 212.

19   Jacques Derrida, *Of Grammatology*, trans. Gayatri Chakrovorty Spivak (Baltimore, Johns Hopkins University Press, 1977), 166.

must be stressed, points to the impossibility of locating the absolute origin of language in either event or structure. Most important, *différance* refers to the impossibility of locating a pure temporal puncture, a present point in time experiences without the overlap and difference of past and future that frame the present.[20] But the key is that *différance* points to the break up of metaphysical self-presence and destroys the pretense of absolute closure in language.

Admittedly, to argue that Irigaray employs a deconstructive strategy to overcome the Lacanian language and logic of male hegemony seems daunting. She must criticize Lacan's language by using that language. Quite simply, she cannot occupy a meta-position outside of language itself. But the Lacanian language has the "power to reduce all others to the economy of the same [and] . . . to eradicate the difference between the sexes in systems that are representative of the masculine subject [indeed] it is impossible to disengage a woman from the current symbolic system."[21] Her strategy, then, is one of mimicry. Specifically, Irigaray plays with the representations of the female body; that is, the biological/cultural body and the body as a discursive construct. She argues, "there is no such thing as a body itself unmediated by textuality."[22] Mimicry then means returning to and repeating "ideas about a woman that are elaborated by the masculine logic but also to make visible by an effect of playful repetition what was to remain invisible."[23]

To frame her discussion of a woman's body, I shall begin with her repetition of the Lacanian reading of the Oedipus Complex, returning again to the mirror phase and the *fort/da* game. The central question in this critique is, "How can a woman's difference be reclaimed?" Irigaray begins by attacking Lacan's descriptions of the metaphysical ground of male subjectivity. As indicated above, she finds this ground in Lacan's valorization of the womb. This is a negative value—women are cast as an object-body. The result is that a woman (M)other is consigned to immanence with the body. Irigaray says Lacan's description of the womb is part of his attempt to reconstruct the first dwelling of the child and to see in the male child's developmental stages evidence of recovery from separation and male mastery. This is crucial because it sets into motion a

---

[20] Jacques Derrida, *Positions* (Chicago: University of Chicago Press, 1981), 28.

[21] Irigaray, *The Sex, Which Is Not One*, 27.

[22] Ibid., 133.

[23] Ibid., 16.

subject/object separation, the logic that drives the Oedipal Conflict. Again, for Irigaray, Lacan's reading is a metaphysical misrecognition. She argues that to reconstruct the first dwelling is impossible. The placental veil between mother and child has been destroyed and cannot be reconstituted. But what is important is neither the child's nor the mother's separateness; the placenta is both his and hers, neither fully nor clearly one before birth.[24] In this light, recasting the mirror phase, Irigaray says, "to have access to a woman is not the desire for the father's power, but rather the desire to return to this primal home, which leads [the male infant] to conflate the destroyed . . . placenta with the mirror in which he sees himself whole and intact."[25]

The upshot of this wholeness is to misrecognize her; she is not a transcendent subject, but a fluid object of immanence. The child's desire to suture his separation, together with his inability to accept the fluidity of embodiment, allows him to equate femininity with the body. The mirror image proclaims his mastery in the specularity of his gaze. Again, the medium of this drama is the male transcendental gaze, which is reflected in a mirror of misrecognition. In sum, male specular self, who seems whole and intact, singular and powerful, finds its cultural exemplar in the phallus. But Irigaray's rereading presents a relationship of the mother and child that has no sharp demarcations. The metaphor of conflict is replaced with the metonymy of juncture; separation becomes ambiguous. This becomes the theme of Irigaray's deconstruction of the phallus in her discussion of the labia.

Irigaray's stress on the female genitalia is meant to expose the absolute presence of the phallus by introducing difference to this linguistic transcendental signifier. That is, she intends to defer and displace this original seemingly permanent phallus signifier; therefore, she focuses on the labia to expose the protean possibilities of the language. Irigaray's strategy is to employ deconstruction to break up the self-presence of the phallus, thereby denying it the possibility of an ultimate meaning and power in the phallus.

The phallus represents the politics of a woman's erasure and her muted voice of subordination. Anatomy is destiny and nature legislates women's predestination as a being who is the same as, but a deficient man. How then can Irigaray recover women's difference, her voice and identity? Her move is to play the male's game—that is, to embrace

---

[24] Ibid.
[25] Ibid.

anatomy as her answer. Of course, this strategy is controversial. Opposed to the phallus, she inscribes the female lips as the mark of a woman's difference.

The obvious objections to this move are its logic and its seeming essentialism. To apparently inscribe women's lips as the transcendental signifier is to conform to the binary logic of the phallus. That is, if Irigaray is to give a woman an identity, it must fail. Why? A completed woman's subjectivity once again articulates the language of closure and, therefore, fits into the scopic economy: a woman is reinstated as the same deficient male. Yet, emphasizing the lips seems to be a form of essentialism in which biology determines sexual identity; this again would reinforce a woman as absence.

Space does not permit a full elaboration of her rebuttal of the Lacanian paradigm. It is sufficient to say that Irigaray excavates blind spots in the psychoanalytic economy. These include a failure to be self-reflexive regarding methodology, a misplaced emphasis on the clitoris in the explanation of psychosexual development, a lack of understanding regarding the plural sites of female sexual pleasure, and ultimately, a metaphysical description of women, which under the guise of nature, is really ahistorical.

How then does Irigaray show women's lips as the mark of difference? Her answer is deliberately ambiguous. Women's lips have a dual meaning; the lips point at once to the biological and the symbolic realms. In biological terms, the lips refer to the mouth and the female genitalia, i.e., the labia. Equally important, her lips, as part of a woman's body, are sexually marked within the male scopic economy. The point to be emphasized is that the body is always already interpreted. Again, women's sexuality is defined as both an empirical reality and as a discursive construct—a text.[26] But a careful reading of Irigaray shows that the lips are neither an oppositional transcendental signifier nor the empirical body itself. That is, Irigaray does not speak of the lips to denote an indexical or existential relationship to the empirical body. Her usage of lips is meant to connote a morphological set of meanings that draws attention to formal resemblances.[27] Remember her subversive strategy is one of mimicry.

Mimicry puts into relief Irigaray's analysis of language, the male

---

[26] Kaja Silverman, The Subject of Semiotics (New York and London: Oxford University Press), 19.
[27] Irigaray, *This Sex Which Is Not* One, 212.

scopic economy, a woman's body and the lips. Regarding the need for a feminine language of difference, she says, "If we keep on speaking the same language together, we're going to reproduce the same history." Regarding male specularity, a woman confronts a mirage: "A (scarcely) living mirror [into which] she/it is frozen, mute . . . into bodies already encoded with a system. [Men have] left us only lacks, deficiencies, to designate ourselves."[28] On a woman's body, there is

> no event that makes us women. Long before your birth you touched yourself innocently. Your/my body doesn't acquire its sex through an operation, the action of some power, function, or organ. Without any intervention . . . you are a woman already. [And in still another pointed attack on Lacan's Mirror Phase.] There is no need for an outside [mirror], the other already affects you.[29]

But, the pivotal descriptions are those of the lips: "our two lips cannot separate to let just one word pass. A single word that would say, 'you' or 'me' . . . closed and open, neither ever excluding the other . . . to produce a single precise word, they would have to stay apart. Definitely parted kept at a distance, separated by one word without lips, there is no more 'us.' Open your lips . . . we—you/I—are neither open nor closed. We never separate simply: a single word cannot be pronounced, produced, uttered by our mouths."[30] Throughout, difference is expressed in the tension between terms that comprise an evolving language of and for a woman.

Irigaray's descriptions of a woman's lips have a multilayered significance for her philosophy of difference. Thematically, difference is exposed between sexual and discursive identity, specularity, touch, and ethics. The crucial point again is that the sexual connotations of lips refer both to biological and cultural definitions. In biological terms, lips refer both to the mouth and the labia. In cultural terms, a woman's lips are not only marked sexually, they are the source of her speech and her discursive definition (such as the one seen in Lacan). But, the parting and closing of the lips connotes more than speech or sexual pleasure. What is central is the opening and closing of the lips as physical/discursive sites of the body. Crucially, the emphasis on opening/closing and touching

---

[28] C.f. Kaja Silverman, The Subject of Semiotics (New York and London. Oxford University Press), 19.
[29] Irigaray, *This Sex Which Is Not One,* 212.
[30] Ibid.

underscores the importance of a space between. This opening, this negative space with its lack of demarcation yet unity, with the touching of lips, is meant to describe the possibility of women's unalienated relationships toward each other. Their unalienated relationship cannot be circumscribed by the apparent physical separation of boundaries.

In sum, lips are the difference in opposition to the phallus. The fixity of the specularized male subject is different from the unbounded touching of a woman whose subjectivity is not individualized and remains a work in progress.

In the final section, I shall set down the conditions of the dialogical encounter that Irigaray believes are necessary to ethical reflection and the transformation of culture, and the creation of a new female dialogical subject.

What has been seen above is an attack on phallocentrism, with its legitimation of male political hegemony in the specular regime. Western philosophical history finds the fulfillment of this ideology in the transcendental subjectivity appearing with Kant and most recently reproduced by Lacan. A woman in this discursive practice is reduced to the deficient sameness of man. How does Irigaray propose to escape the prison house of the phallocentric Symbolic Order? Her answer lies in an examination of the dialogical relationship. Beginning with the morphology of the female body, she moves to a dialectic of reversibility, from which a double subjectivity emerges.

The morphology of the female body is summed up in the phrase, "*L'incontournable volume,*" which Iragary emphasizes must be translated as an open volume—one that cannot be circumscribed; a body which is fluid and permeable[31] This is the body previously described as having space which is neither inside nor outside, but both simultaneously. Following rediscussion of lips, the body is neither social/empirical nor discursive, but both. The body morphology in this sense eludes the subject/object separation. Some sense of this reality is found in the activity of washing one's hands. As I wash my left hand with my right, the left becomes an object. Switching hands, my left hand washing makes the right hand the object of washing. But all the while both hands are inseparable from my subjectivity. Subject and object are in a dialectical reversal or crossover in Merleau-Ponty's terms, a crossover or

---

[31] Luce Irigaray, "Je-Luce Irigaray": A Meeting With Luce Irigaray, in *Hypathia: A Journal of Feminist Philosophy,* 10, no. 2, (Spring 1995): 98.

chiasm.[32]

Indeed, Irigaray's double subjectivity stresses the relationship to the other. She says, "it is important to me not only to say, 'I' but to say I-she (Je elle)."[33] This is a subjectivity that expresses itself in a dialectic between subjectivity and objectivity. Then, "I myself write, 'I,' as 'I' marked 'she' (Je indice elle), which permits me to make visible that the subject is two, that is not a unique subject, and to pose all sorts of dialogic questions."[34] Remember, an intersection between two different subjects became possible out of the "'*L'incontrounable volume*' of the body that replaces the specular subjectivity." Irigaray warns that "this 'I' must be a dialogical, 'I' must not be . . . [a] purely narrative autobiographical 'I' [nor one of pure affect]. Because such an 'I' reverts to . . . pathos [the I] the woman also uses in her place, the home."[35] Irigaray wants a sexed feminine "I"; to get there "it's necessary to remain in both objective and subjective."[36]

But her use of the pronoun "I" differs according to text. At one moment it emphasizes a refusal to "dictate truth for others." At another moment, it becomes a deconstructive strategy to breakup the traditional male philosophical subject who dictates the truth."[37]

Her task is to enounce a double utterance [*une parole a'deux*] that would respect the "I" and "You." But always the truth elicited is a sensible truth— "one that changes with experience."[38] Her final warning is that she "can't affirm that this is always already the experience of a woman. It must be a dialectic between subjectivity and objectivity."[39]
Lip service has been given to the language of "political correctness" as a model which schools should embrace in order to promote equity and respect for all. In the face of a culture whose popular media exposes children to behaviors and language that emphasize women as acceptable victims of violence, such rhetoric is hollow. Other feminists, most notably Carol Gilligan, have argued that the schools in their discursive practices perpetuate the formation of girls who will become women

---

[32] Irigiary's discussion obviously is deeply influenced by Merleau-Ponty's phenomenology of perception.
[33] Ibid, 103.
[34] Ibid.
[35] Ibid.
[36] Ibid.
[37] Ibid., 104.
[38] Ibid.
[39] Ibid.

without a political voice. Irigaray argues that women must make history and language itself. Finally, it must be emphasized that Irigaray is well aware that the "definition" of a woman changes according to her color, economic status, and citizenship. Her Marxist inspired criticisms of women as commodities inscribe this view.[40] Irigaray's dialogical model presents hope for a new sociocultural order of difference, a reclamation of a woman's subjectivity, and a new theoretical paradigm for educational practice. The next chapter presents Julia Kristeva's technique of reading that builds on Irigaray's critique. Chapter Nine teases out of the condition of woman as a being without a voice and a model of reading that captures the politically emancipatory possibilities contained in the unreadable texts of sexual bliss (*jouissance*).

---

[40]   Ibid. 138.

Chapter 9
Kristeva:
Reading with *Jouissance*

Ironically, anecdotal evidence from my experience teaching multicultural studies is that for many students, the feminist political critique today seems outdated and without personal relevance for their daily lives. The consensus is that the position of women has been bettered and "the culture has arrived at closure regarding women's rights; therefore, we must move on to other things."

My view is that this argument is both wrong and politically repressive. Having said that, I shall argue that the anti-feminist ideology is insinuated within our teaching practices, indeed it fills our ordinary language practices—in novels, for example. I argue that the anti-feminist ideology is rampant, because it is embedded in the unconscious and is expressed in the language we use; that language is one with self-definition or subjectivity. Building on what has already been seen in Irigaray, I seek to split the subjectivity by exposing protocols of reading a text of erotic bliss. My task, then, is to search for pedagogical protocols of reading that will change minds.

This critique turns to Julia Kristeva's postfeminist destabilization of the Lacanian *Symbolic Order*. Central here is her distinction between the *symbolic* and the *semiotic,* as well as her constructs of the *abject* and *chora.* This is joined in Barthes' technique of reading, called *jouissance,* which is a mechanism of ideology critique. All of the above are put into play in the reading of Marguerite Duras' feminist novel, *The Lover.* The intent is twofold: first, to provide a specific novel as a model for multicultural pedagogy; second, to treat the novel as a metaphorical body, showing how a rechanneling of the reader's own bodily experience of *bliss* also provides new political understanding.[1] Specifically, my concern is to split the homogenous subjectivity constructed by the patriarchal culture, so that new gendered positions can be opened. With Lacan as its start, my critique moves to Julia Kristeva, Roland Barthes, and then to Marguerite Duras. Again, a brief review of Lacan's key words puts the discussion in context.[2]

What is of particular interest is the Lacanian stage called "The Symbolic." For Lacan, the resolution of the Oedipus Conflict is previewed by the child's acquisition of language. This is the Symbolic stage, in which language is a substitute satisfaction meant to appease the child's separation from mother. Language then is the site of lack and desire; Lacan argues that the unconscious itself is structured like language. If language allows the child to call forth "mama" in her physical absence, language then also places the child into the culture's preexisting fields of discourse. Language articulates that set of relationships, known as the subject.[3] The child's entrance into language is an initiation into what Lacan calls the "Name of the Father," or "The Symbolic Order," which constitutes all the signs, linguistic and otherwise, that represent the institutions of the culture. Gender bias is built into the Symbolic Order; through it, the male child gains unity, identity, and ultimately full partnership in the cultural patriarchy. This symbol of entitlement and control is what Lacan calls the "phallus." The female child, by mimicking biology, is trapped within a linguistic void, where she is missing the copula of being. Lacan concludes the female does not exist. He is not denying the existence of women, but is instead arguing that the female is without subjectivity in the Symbolic Order.

---

1   Bliss is used synonymously with the French j*ouissance* to denote an orgasmic experience. The translator uses the term "coming" to specify the meaning for English speakers.

2   See Jacques Lacan, *The Four Fundamental Concepts of Psychoanalysis*, trans. Alan Sheridan (New York: W.W. Norton & Company, 1978).

3   To call the subject split invokes the psychoanalytic Oedipal Stage of an embodied sexual being, i.e., the subject is cut between the primary process of the unconscious/libido and the secondary process of consciousness.

To see the use of Lacan for a multicultural feminist reading model, I shall now turn to the feminist philosopher, Julia Kristeva.

In agreement with Lacan, Kristeva argues that the Symbolic Order (what she calls "the socio-symbolic contract") is based on sexual difference. She argues that although the girl lacks the penis and is without representation in the Symbolic Order, this must not be taken as an acceptance of political destiny. The female's lack, as opposed to the male's phallic completion, is an ideological mystification. For Kristeva, "the Symbolic Order must never be accepted, and never ignored. The female subject is neither transcendental nor erased, but subversively at odds with what exists."[4]

If the subject is constituted by language, Kristeva argues that no sociopolitical change is possible for women, unless there is a change in the relationship of the subject to language.

Kristeva's attack on the social contract of the Symbolic Order rethinks language use, showing how the female's representation as a lack can be turned into an instrument of ideological critique. She argues that our understanding of language use must be expanded from thinking that it is merely a thetic operation. Instead, language is described as having two necessary and interdependent modalities: the symbolic and the semiotic. This distinction is crucial because it recasts the subject into a set of identity relationships that can be changed. In Kristeva's words, the subject is a "subject in process."

In her distinction, the symbolic function is one of predication: the subject of the sentence, the copula, and the predicate; i.e., "John is a man." In the symbolic function there is a clear attribution between the meaning of a signifier, "John," and the signified class, "man." The symbolic level is one of fully articulated language of representations and images.

By contrast, the semiotic level represents the poet's playing with language. For example, in Joyce's *Ulysses,* Molly Bloom's soliloquy ends:

---

[4]   See Julia Kristeva, *The Revolution in Poetic Language*, trans. Margaret Waller, (New York: Columbia University Press 1984). See also Mary Lydon, "The Forgetfulness of Memory: Jacques Lacan, Marguerite Duras, and the Text," *Contemporary Literature* 36: 3. 1982.

160

> "He asked me would I say yes to say yes my mountain flower and first I put my arms around him yes and drew him down to me so he could feel my breasts all perfume yes and his heart was going like mad and I said yes I will yes."[5]

Obviously here is the delight of repetition in the rhythm of the word combinations themselves. Reading Joyce is like singing, surrendering to word play and the joy of sounds one hears in the head. If the semiotic is not the predicative, but the lyrical function of language, its foundation can be heard originally in the infant's echolalic play and echolalia in Joyce:

> "What sounds did Bloom, diambulist, father of Milly, somnabulist, make to Stephen noctambulist?" is reconstituted as art.[6]

The sounds said, or heard in the head, their echolalic rhythms and emotional tonalities, are that part of language that does not name, but nonetheless is integral to, language use. Kristeva argues that the semiotic is the feminine, the unnamable material dimension of language. To call the semiotic feminine and unnamable reinstates Lacan's construct of the female as the site of loss, a subject without copula, divided—a void. But here is Kristeva's crucial twist, absence, lack, the unrepresentable of the semiotic is the unnamable place called the chora. "Heterogeneous to meaning, the chora animates the flow of *jouissance* of the body that constitutes desire. The chora opens a fault in language, which shows what lies beyond the limits of the naming function. The chora rips apart the Symbolic Order, revealing the illusory description of the homogeneous, complete subject. In its place is the confrontation with the instinctual drive of the chora, the semiotization of language that happens in art."[7] Art, in Kristeva's sense, utters the unutterable; in doing so it reveals the subject as a subject in process. Giving in to the play of semiosis represents the possibility of the subject's self-reflection, as a subject divided, in process of becoming. This recognition has the revolutionary potential to reconstitute the Symbolic Order.

The condition produced in the subject is what Kristeva calls the

---

[5] James Joyce, *Ulysses* (New York: The Modern Library, 1961), 783.
[6] Ibid., p. 27. See also Philip E. Lewis, "The Revolutionary Semiotics," *Diacritics* 4 (1974), 31., and Catherine Marchak, "The Joy of Transgression," *Philosophy Today*, (Winter 1990). Marchak describes the chora as the presymbolic receptacle of the maternal body.
[7] Julia Kristeva, *The Revolution in Poetic Language*, 84–96.

"abject."[8] This unsettling of the subject, this refusal of closure, highlights societal prohibitions for the subject, which she/he can no longer obey. No longer "clean and sober," the subject searches for pleasures that go beyond the Symbolic Order, a pleasure that Roland Barthes also describes as *jouissance*.

Thus far, the argument has outlined the relationship between language, the unconscious, and the Symbolic Order in the construction of gender. The Kristeva discussion depicted the liberation potential of semiosis: poetry's semiosis pushes the reader to question the symbolic limits of language and one's own subjectivity. Kristeva calls this an erotic state, a condition in which the reader surrenders to his/her *jouissance*. While both Kristeva and Barthes employ the construct of *jouissance,* specific attention will be given to Barthes' use of the term. To contextualize *jouissance*, a brief discussion of the novel's narrativity and representation follow.

Scholes defines narrativity as "the process by which the perceiver constructs a story from fictional data; [further] narrativity involves a process in which any representational medium will construct a chain of events moving toward a *telos*."[9] It is through narrativity that the reader moves from ignorance to knowledge; narrativity is the pleasurable movement toward the novel's resolution or closure. Narrativity presents the reader with the coherent sequence of beginning, middle, and end.

Representations or events are stages in the narrative that "make sense," because of the reader's performance of giving words meaning. What is crucial, though, is that the reader sustains the narrative by giving coherence, logic, and completion, thereby allowing the reader to construct a coherent and complete subjectivity. That is, the images of the novel are what the reader/subject interpellates, producing the self.[10]

Typically, the conventional novel confers pleasure; but it is a pleasure that reflects a subjectivity *channeled through cultural discourses* that sustain the political sexist *status quo*. It must be emphasized that pleasure is not the bliss of *jouissance*. Barthes wants to create a different reading experience, one in which the reader and author

---

8   See Julia Kristeva, *Powers of Horror, An Essay in Abjectio,* trans. Leon S. Roudiez. (New York: Columbia University Press, 1980).

9   See Robert Scholes, *Textual Power* (New Haven: Yale University Press, 1985).

10   Leslie Fiedler argues that the novel's origins answered the need of the merchant classes for a model of propriety. See Leslie Fiedler, *Love and Death in the American Novel* (New York: Stein and Day, 1966).

positions are displaced; the death of the author means the birth of the reader.

The first condition necessary is the selection of a proper text. To induce *jouissance,* the novel must be one that challenges the reader, forcing an overthrow of habitual ways of reading; the reader must confront obstacles in his/her reading. That kind of novel is called a *self-reflexive text*—one that forces the reader to pay attention to the organizing function of the narrative. Barthes contrasts the self-reflexive text of *jouissance* against pleasurable work. The pleasurable work as already indicated mimes the ordinary taken-for-granted world. Barthes calls the pleasurable work this is an expression of, the natural attitude and the novel's device, which produces that attitude of *vraisemblance.*

The natural attitude works as an ideological device, a representation of reality that serves the class interests of dominant groups by sustaining sexist political relations as normal. That is, the natural attitude delivers a picture of the world, together with one's place in it; this is a practice that delivers images, behaviors, and attitudes that form and sustain not only one's place, but one's belief in the socioeconomic hierarchy. Ultimately, the work of ideological practice fixes human beings into certain reified modes of discourse. That is, the social world becomes intelligible as complete and unchanging, and the *present social-political hierarchy appears natural because signifiers of the language are concealed to certain signifieds.* For example, in the postmodern capitalist ideology, political conservatism signifies patriotism, federal welfare projects signify socialism, and homophobia signifies a rite of purification.

The natural attitude is insinuated in the novel as *vraisemblance,* an accurate, truthful, natural copy. That is, the possibility of sense-making is delivered to the reader by certain conventions of interpretation, certain "modes of order which culture makes available, and this is usually done by talking about [the novel] in a mode of discourse which culture takes as natural."[11] Heath calls the convention of *vraisemblance* "the text of the natural attitude of a society, entirely familiar and in this very familiarity diffuse, unknown as a text."[12] *Vraisemblance* tries to make the reader "believe that the text conforms to reality and not its own laws.

---

[11] Roland Barthes, "L'Ancienne Rh'etorique: Aide M'emorie." *Communication,* 16, 1970. p. 12. For a phenomenological description, see Edmund Husserl, *Ideas,* trans. W.R. Boyce Gibson (London: Collier Books, 1969), 96.

[12] Stephen Heath, *The Noveau Roman* (Philadelphia: Temple University Press, 1972), 21.

But *vraisemblance* is the mask concealing the text's own laws which the reader is supposed to take for a relation with reality. Barthes says the text's laws represent the discourse of the natural attitude, a discourse that requires no justification because it seems to derive directly from the structure of the world. *Vraisemblance,* then, is the cultural grid against which the novel both gains meaning and defines the logic of human actions. The point of arguing that the ideology of the natural attitude is one with the *vraisemblance* of the ordinary novel is that the reader introjects a politically loaded message in the act of reading. To provide evidence, I shall now turn to Barthes' treatment of the subjectivity of the reader. He says:

> Subjectivity is generally thought of as a plentitude with which I encumber the text, but in fact this fake plentitude is only that wash of all the rodes which make up the "I": so that finally, my subjectivity has the generality of stereotypes.[13]

To split this unified structure of subjectivity, Barthes demands that we listen to our inner voice; this is the "I" in dialogue, with the narrator of the novel as we read it. Reading involves not only encoding and decoding, but it also involves speaking and listening to one's self. In reading, the "I" enters into a dialogue with the text's narrator—a narrator who speaks to me and all other imaginary interlocutors, with words that transform the "I." Quite simply, the reader, this "I," disappears in the textual dialogue of reading and "becomes" the narrator.

What the narrator/reader has become is an observer who makes the text intelligible, telling the reader which things are important, what the world is like, and giving a linear-sequential order to textual events. The narrator, though, "I," is also formed. The reader is told how to think, how to react, and how to judge the unfolding scene. This vision and these values appear natural and normal. They are, however, political statements to the question, "Who speaks this dialogue?" Barthes answers, "what is heard is the *displaced voice*," this "I," is the construction of the text.[14] However, this is "I"; the reader is a hypostatized observer, the social construction of an ideological practice.

A false conclusion to be drawn from this critique is that the reader must necessarily become the victim of ideological practice. Barthes

---

[13]   Roland Barthes, *S/Z*, (Paris: Sevil, 1973), 16–17.
[14]   Ibid.

argues that choosing a different kind of text, not one that induces the comfortable pleasure of familiarity, but a text and a practice that is the site of the reader's *jouissance,* can expose ideological practice.

To set the stage for Barthes' arguments, a summary of what has been shown and implied about the subject "I" reader follows. First, the subject is not really a completed entity, but a subject created in the process of signification in the dialectic of institutional practices. Second, it has been argued that this subject in process is a split self, a self that is cut. Calling the subject split is to invoke a psychoanalytic description of the subject; i.e., the subject is a being cut between the primary process of the unconscious or libido and the secondary process of consciousness—the arena of substitute satisfactions. The original split refers to that milestone that announces the child's entrance into language and the Symbolic Order. Freud's paradigm case of the child's symbolic play with the physically absent mother, using the words "here" (*fort*) and "there," (*da*) denotes an emblematic satisfaction and loss. The site of loss, the cut, is at once the place of satisfaction—bliss. This psychoanalytic model is the ground for the discussion of *jouissance.* Reprising Freud's model of the "here" and "there" game, the adult's *jouissance* in reading represents the dialectic of desire, an act of simultaneous satisfaction and loss. Barthes says the site of *jouissance* has two edges.[15] This is what Barthes variously calls the seam, the cut, the fault, the perforation, the break, or the intermittence. This means one reaches *jouissance* not through the coy manipulations of a stagy striptease, but through the glimpses of the hidden body, the human body, and the textual body. The eroticized human body tantalizes, showing itself where the garment parts. These are the edges where articles of clothing meet and separate. This is the intermittence of skin flashing between the trousers and sweater, the glove and the sleeve, or the open-necked shirt.

Barthes applies this sexual arousal metaphorically to the novel. Treating the novel as a body—as the site of libidinal satisfaction— Barthes carefully distinguishes between the readable novel of pleasure and the unreadable novel of *jouissance.* The pleasurable work has a silky aerodynamic, a "zero degree drag coefficient" of euphoria. Reading the novel of pleasure allows the reader to participate in the cultural story, and comforts him/her through the fullness and consistency of their subjectivity as a complete "I." The text of pleasure is a text without tears

---

15   Roland Barthes, *The Pleasure of the Text*, trans. Richard Miller (New York: Hill and Wang, 1975), 7.

or cuts. For example, Agatha Christie's novels give the reader the text of pleasure: she creates a bucolic bourgeois world in which the suspense of "whodunit" plays itself out through a gradual unveiling.

On the opposite edge, however, the text of *jouissance* presents an erotics of loss, discomfort, and even boredom. Such a text unsettles "the reader's historical, cultural, [and] psychological assumptions, [as well as] the consistency of his tastes, values, [and] memories, [bringing] to a crisis his relation with language."[16]

The text of *jouissance* is a patchwork of cuts; this is a discourse so ripped with perforations that the text of reading is turned inside out. Barthes cites the commingling of antithetical codes, a device used by the Marquis de Sade, to make a point. By reading de Sade, one finds a mixture of the trivial and the elevated—together, obscene content is presented in "sentences so pure, they might be used as grammatical models." This tear turns reading inside out because the places of the reader and writer have been dislodged. "There is not behind in the text someone active (the writer); there is not a subject and object."[17] Instead, the text of *jouissance* forces the reader to make sense without the benefits of *vraisemblance:* such pleasurable works allow the reader to receive images and to bask in the reproduction of the culture's unquestioned images and belief systems. Pleasurable works have a logical coherence and a familiar spatio-temporal order.

By contrast, the text of *jouissance* breaks down the encoding process, and it is simply words themselves that stand out on the page. In place of logical coherence, the reader confronts disjointed strips of action; like the writer, the reader is forced to shift and collect elements of the novel together. This is not simply a tying of pieces together; instead, the reader is pushed to pay attention to the disjointed and even missing forms that construct any novel. There is no closure, only a rearranging of strips of narrative.

Such a reading practice is finally the overturning of ideological practice. The reader subject created in *jouissance* is in crisis where she/he is a split self. Such a reader is forced to use the accustomed language of domination in new ways: the task of reading, the object of reading, and the reader becomes self-reflexive data. Over and against the text of *jouissance,* the reader now sees the ideological seams in

---

[16] Ibid., 14.
[17] Roland Barthes, *Critical Essays* (Evanston: Northwestern University Press, 1972), 150.

166

signification appearing on other texts of experience. The reader comes to his orgasm as an active self-creative subject in the process of confronting the natural attitude. Pedagogically, the student translates the unnamable experience of cultural sexism. The question then becomes, how can this be taught?

The problem is to find an appropriate text. While there are many possibilities, the choice of a paradigm text of feminist *jouissance* must satisfy a number of criteria. The novel must expose the reader to the politics of his/her gender codification, be self-reflexive, thereby showing how the narration organizes the reader's subjectivity, and in its self-reflexivity, the text must alienate the reader. The semiotic play of language must be recovered; the reader's pleasure must be overturned and she/he must be brought to the unnamable state of abjection through *jouissance*. With these criteria in mind, any number of texts can be chosen. The choice of a conventional, *pleasurable* text could be used to highlight the ideology of female domination. My own choice, however, is Marguerite Duras' novel as a paradigm text of *jouissance*.[18]

The daughter of French colonials, Madame Duras was raised in the prewar twenties of Indochina. A controversial playwright and filmmaker, her reputation was first established as a member of the French feminist writer's group called *Ecriture Feminine*.

The Lover is a thinly veiled autobiography, which became an international bestseller that was later made into a film. It is placed in the years prior to the Japanese invasion of Indochina, and is the story of a *tabooed* interracial love affair between the French fifteen-year-old child-narrator, and an adult Chinese financier, set against a background of her family trauma. At its core, this is a story of *sexual love, loss, and the deconstruction of subjectivity*. It is a self-reflexive novel, a paradigm of *jouissance*. What follows are sketches of *jouissance* from the reading of the text. *The Lover* includes the following narrative devices: central characters who are themselves abject, the use of repetitive descriptions, the disturbance of narrativity, and the focus on irrelevant detail. Abjection is introduced in the description of sexual identities which are

---

[18] Marguerite Duras. *The Lover,* trans. Barbara Bray (New York: Pantheon Books, 1985). Some have argued that the choice of this novel expresses an elitist attitude. The text was written by a French colonial in a style unusual for the typical reader. My response is that the choice was dictated by the need to provide the reader with a self-reflexive text of bliss that exposes the ideological work of constructing the subject.

not quite socially acceptable. The teenage narrator dresses as she wants to be seen—a weird, little tart. She mixes a worn, transparent dress with a plunging neckline, *lamé* high heels, and a man's belt and fedora. Stripped of his expensive suit, the man seems almost feminine; his skin is "sumptuously" soft and hairless, and his body is thin and lacks muscle. There is nothing masculine about him, except his sex.[19] Abjection is reinforced with the rumors about this liaison between a disenfranchised poor girl and the *noveau riche* politically connected man. Neither side of the social and racial divide will publicly speak about such a union; discourse is absent. The abject condition of the narrator is underlined as she seduces him and demands payment for sex. This reversal of the conventional narrator's role is a foretaste of what is to come in the controlling images of the novel: the narrator's self-description is a theme with variations. Duras writes: "I often think of the image only I can see now, and of which I've never spoken."[20]

> It's on a ferry crossing the Mekong River. The girl in the felt hat is in the muddy light of the river, on the deck of the ferry . . .
> Fifteen and a half. The news spread fast in Sadec. The clothes she wears are enough to show. The mother has no idea, and none about how to bring up a daughter. Don't tell me that that's innocent.
> Every morning the little slut goes to have her body caressed by a filthy, Chinese millionaire.[21]

Notice how the disruption of the narrator's voice with each repetition is like a musical chord change. The pronominal "I" in "I often think," is changed into the objective, "*The girl* in the hat"; "The clothes *she* wears" is finally changed into the self-descriptor, "little slut." Abjection would be complete if it were not for Duras' defiance. This repetitive theme, these cool descriptions of pain and pleasure, the musicality of these sounds, this semiosis represents a recollection that Duras has *never uttered,* but which she now writes. This is an attack on gender codification and its subordination positioning of women; in the conventional novel, the older man would be dominant, the seducer, not the seduced. Though outside the Name of the Father and the Law, such a story would reinforce the morality of the Symbolic Order. *The Lover,* however, derives its real power in naming this unnamable.

---

[19] Ibid., 38.
[20] Ibid., 3.
[21] Ibid., 5, 88, 89.

The reader's disorientation builds as the narrator charts the dissolution of her family life in its historical context, including the Japanese occupation of Indochina. The theme is one of horrible *loss,* represented by her mother's madness and the deaths of her two brothers. Her abject condition is marked by irrelevant detail, and the same repetitive image that was encountered before is followed by blank spaces and then a new disconnected recollection. This is the chora, testing the limits of symbolic language. Some examples: in the middle of repeating the image of the ferry on the Mekong, the narrator switches to a detailed description of a photograph, which is an image that is irrelevant to the action. She says, "I found a photograph of my son when he was twenty. He's in California with his friends."[22] In the following paragraph, we are told, "I'm four years old. My mother's in the middle of the picture."[23] Two pages later, the following appears: "I've still got my hair. Fifteen and a half."[24]

There are *cuts, holes in the fabric of story coherence, temporal sequencing is without order. There is no beginning, middle, and end. There are no techniques of vraisemblance* at work. The narrator/reader confronts an unreadable text.

The reader, however, moves from the confusing narrative of the text and questions the ways in which the ordinary practice of reading channels the meanings of the world. As the text breaks apart under the reader's gaze, it shows how the text is made and how it makes meaning. Again, *jouissance* comes from an attention to, and reordering of, internal relationships in the text. There are no final answers; there is only the differal of *petit-mort,* or ejaculations, and a cry of defiance.

In conclusion, my intent was to present a set of protocols that express an emancipatory model of feminist critique. The task is to reach students at the level of their taken-for-granted experience of reading a novel. *The Lover* was chosen because it allows the reader an aesthetic distance while she/he participates in the break up of taken-for-granted understandings, which grasps the way the delivered sexist picture of the world becomes intelligible. She/he overturns the natural attitude by teaching herself how to read and rewrite the world and its possibilities. This is a model of pedagogy intended for my students' bliss. This is the practice of reading called *jouissance.*

---

[22]   Ibid., 13.
[23]   Ibid.
[24]   Ibid., 16.

Epilogue

The intent of this text was to provide new ways of reading the political construction of subjectivity that is embedded in pedagogical discourses. The choice of poststructuralist French thinkers was not only motivated by the inherent attraction of mining their discoveries, but it was also an attempt to expose the dialogue between them. This was underlined by tracing the direction from existential-phenomenology and Marxism to structuralism and then poststructuralism.

Merleau-Ponty's description of Cézanne laid out themes that would recur throughout the text: aesthetics, the body, the perceptual gaze, and Saussure's model of language. For Merleau-Ponty, the subject is autonomous. Chapter Two moves to Saussure's structuralist model, adapted by Levi-Strauss and Lacan, which emphasized a new direction: the subject is depicted as a construction of language that has been subjected to cultural myth. Employing Jacques Lacan's psychoanalytic techniques of reading the unconscious, to Dewey's essay, "The School and Social Progress," demonstrated the latter's work as an American cultural myth. Behind Lacan's analysis lay the separation of the child from the mother during the birth event, and the child's never-ending quest for unity found in substitute satisfactions. In Lacan, the pivotal use of perception and the body were located in the Imaginary or Mirror Phase. Chapter Three extended Lacan's Imaginary to expose Althusser's neo-Marxist critique of the Afrocentric Myth. Removed from phenomenological concerns, the subject is subsumed under the category of production as human labor power.

Chapter Four presented a different take on the theme of myth, this time as it appealed to Barthes' analysis of what culture describes as *natural.* First considered was the American ideology of Equal Opportunity, which was followed by an analysis of another Deweyan myth: the pedagogical discourses of history for the elementary schoolchild. In Chapter Five, the formalism of the structuralist, binary model was rejected by the poststructuralist Foucault, whose aesthetic critique, though still linguistic, presents a new method of excavating the power and political significance of standardized testing in the schools.

In contradiction to Foucault, and appealing to Baudrillard, Chapter Six treated another of Dewey's pedagogical myths as constructions that have no referent in the world. Chapter Seven focused on American racism, as it is directed toward African-Americans and other minorities, as well as cultural pluralist remedies. Both issues are addressed by Derrida's constructs of *différance,* the *supplement,* and *grafting.* Again, this is a critique within a critique, as Derrida employs the phenomenology of the gaze (found in Sartre) and then reveals how deconstruction is an attack on Husserl's constructions of time-consciousness and the *eidos.* All of which inhere in the activity of perception—which Derrida claims is always already an interpretation of experience. Chapter Eight presented Irigaray's deconstruction of phallocentrism. By describing a woman's body as both an empirical reality and discursive construct, she illumines sexual difference and sets the stage for Kristeva's critical model. The final chapter provided Irigaray and Kristeva's Postfeminist model of critique when joined to Barthes, who has left the constraints of a Formalist Structuralism.

In each of the above chapters, the categories employed were designed to illuminate and critique the political dimension of subjectivity formed in the classroom. The desire has been not to find final answers, but to present methods and categories that inform the pedagogical encounter.

Throughout this investigation, a dominant theme has been a reading of the politics of the body. The movement has been one that has focused on the lived body, the specular body, and the discursive body. Placed against the categories of the Symbolic Order, cultural myth, and ideology, the attempt has been one of exposing the mechanisms that mediate and define the pedagogical encounter. The *bricolage* of critical approaches was a deliberate choice, meant to call forth new approaches for an understanding of the school's construction of subjectivity made available in the study of postmodern French thought.

Biographical Notes

Althusser, Louis Pierre (1918–1990). Structuralist Marxist who applied Lacanian imaginary as a paradigm to uncover ideology. *For Marx* (1969).

Barthes, Roland (1915–1980). Poststructuralist whose work uncovered the ideological content in so-called 'natural' cultural phenomena. *Mythologies* (1957).

Baudrillard, Jean (1929-). Poststructuralist social critic who joins linguistic methodology to electronic media, in order to uncover new reality principle-governing culture. *Forget Foucault* (1987).

Derrida, Jacques (1930-). Poststructuralist who assimilates, modifies, and rejects salient elements of phenomenological and structuralist thought. The inventor of deconstruction, he attacks the 'metaphysics of presence,' appearing in traditional attempts to give primacy to the spoken over the written word and final interpretation. *Spurs: Nietzsche's Styles* (1978).

de Saussure, Ferdinand (1857–1913). Inventor of structuralist linguistics, his revolutionary view treated language as having 'differences without positive terms'; i.e., a sign system. *Course in General Linguistics* (1974).

Dewey, John (1859–1952). American philosopher whose instrumentalist model of inquiry was intended as a mode for democracy. The seminal philosopher on American education. *Democracy and Education* (1932).

DuBois, W.E.B. (1868–1963). Afro-American philosopher who helped found the National Association for the Advancement of Colored People. He embraced a Marxist critique as a solution to the racism directed against Afro-Americans. *The Souls of Black Folk* (1903).

Duras, Marguerite (1914–1994). Postfeminist novelist, part of the Nouveau-Roman wave of writers. Her work underscores the failure, cracks, and holes in the work of narration. *Destroy She Said* (1973).

Foucault, Michel (1926–1984). Poststructuralist historian of ideas. Investigations of the human sciences treated the relation between historical changes of thought (epistemes) with practices of power structures. *Archeology of Knowledge* (1972).

Heidegger, Martin (1889–1976). Adapted Husserl's constructs for an ontological investigation of the human being in the world (Dasein). *Being and Time* (1927).

Husserl, Edmund (1859–1938). Inventor of twentieth century phenomenology, major influence on Heidegger, Sartre, Merleau-Ponty; investigated intentional structures of consciousness. *Ideas* (1913).

Irigary, Luce (1930-). Postfeminist who employs critical device of mimicry to expose the philosophical/psychological pretensions that legitimate male political hegemony. *Speculum of the Other Women* (1985).

Kristeva, Julia (1941-). Post-feminist, poststructuralist whose theory of language, "semanalysis," is an important device in the criticism of male hegemony.

Lacan, Jacques (1901–1981). Structuralist psychoanalyst who translated the Freudian unconscious as a language. *Ecrits* (1977).

Levi-Strauss, Claude (1908-). Pioneer in the application of Saussurean structuralist linguistics to an anthropological investigation. *The Elementary Structures of Kinship* (1949).

Lukacs, Georg (1885–1971). His Marxist critique of alienation rejects the explanation of social life as totally derivative of the economic base. His investigations of the subject/object relation emphasized a method of the proletariat seeing its condition as a commodity and thereby acquiring a class consciousness. *History and Class Consciousness* (1923).

Marx, Karl (1818–1883). Most important figure in the history of Western socialist thought. Penetrating analyses of production relationships in the analysis of social and economic class structures. *Capital* (1867).

Merleau-Ponty, Maurice (1908–1961). Existential phenomenologist whose descriptions exposed the meanings of the perceptual act generated by the lived-body. *The Phenomenology of Perception* (1945).

Sartre, Jean Paul (1905–1980). Existential Marxist philosopher whose descriptions focused on individual freedom and choice bounded by situation. *Being and Nothingness* (1943).

Glossary

Abjection: Kristeva's description of the state of unsettling the subject such that she/he no longer accepts certain social prohibitions.

Afrocentrism: Asante's term prescribes a world view, ethical system, history, and religion for Africans worldwide. Suppressed in the West by Eurocentrism.

American Creed: The cultural myth that upward social mobility is available to all, regardless of gender, sexual, religious, or racial background.

Authenticity: Existential-phenomenological term, denoting actions/ choices made in such a way as to embrace one's situation and its possibilities.

Chiasm: Merleau-Pontys term describing the crisscross or reversal that is one with the perceptual act. Perception involves the simultaneity of seeing and being seen.

Chora: Kristeva's term to describe an opening, absence, or fault in language, manifested in literary works; also an unrepresentable site of mother and model of feminist critique.

Commodity fetishism: Marx's term to describe the "mystical" power of commodities in capitalist society to make everything, including humans themselves, appear as things having value, according to the law of supply and demand.

Cultural Myth: Culturally sanctioned ground for understanding the world; also the vehicle of ideology.

Cultural Pluralism: The putative equality of representation of diverse racial/ethnic groups within the school curriculum.

Deconstruction: Derrida's reading strategy used to break apart the final authoritative meaning of a text, showing underlayers of repressed meanings.

Différance: Derrida's description of writing, which rejects the view that a final meaning can be set down; meaning is suspended by difference and the deferral of closure.

En-Soi: Sartre's description of things, not human.

Essence: Husserl's description of ideas as atemporal, unchanging, repeatable entities.

Eubonics: The Afro-American English Language.

Existential Phenomenology: The application of Husserl's paradigm, directed toward a description of the human "being in the world."

Hyper-reality: Baudrillard's term to describe the electronic media culture, which simulates the reproduction of a reproduction. Disneyland, "Venice" in Las Vegas, and photographs of photographs are examples.

Ideological state apparatus (ISA): Althusser's term to describe cultural mechanisms of social formation. Institutions within the ISA mediate, define, and legitimate the socioeconomic class system.

Ideology: A system of ideas/values which, in a critical context, is described as a network of distortions intended to maintain the political hegemony of the ruling class.

Mirror-stage: Lacan's description of the infant's psycho-sexual development, in which his/her reflected image is misrecognized, i.e., the infant believes she/he is an autonomous self. This is an illusion built on a false body image.

Natural Attitude: The uncritical acceptance of experience of the world.

Normalization: Foucault's description of a "scientific" political mechanism that uses totalizing procedures of classification to impose normality and impose remediation. The result is the creation of a certain kind of subjectivity.

Paradigm: Signs that have relations of substitution: John is a rational animal.

Particularism: Any version of Ethnocentric politics.

Pedagogy: The function or work of teaching; in this text specifically, pedagogy is examined as practices that construct subjectivity.

Phallocentrism: Term critically applied to the Freudian/Lacanian primacy given to male hegemony.

Phenomenology: Husserl's twentieth century version is the study of appearing reality, focusing on the modes of consciousness.

Poststructuralism: Adherents simulataneously make use of and criticize the Saussurean Linguistic model. i.e., Derrida, in keeping with the Structuralist Agenda, downplays meaning constituted by conscious subjects, yet, also rejects the Structuralist argument for explicit, formal, and self-sufficient structures.

Pour-soi: Sartre's description of human consciousness as a transcendence of freedom within a situation.

Pre-predicative meaning: Merleau-Ponty's description of meaning generated by the lived-body: neither a reflex nor cognition, but the mean between the two.

Presence: Derrida's description of "all the names related to fundamentals, to principles, or to the center designated [as] an invariable."

Representationalism: The mediation of direct perception through ideational structures.

Semiosis: Kristeva's description of the lyrical function of language; i.e., the rhythm or word combinations and wordplay. This is in contradistinction to the symbolic or the predicative function of language.

Signified: The mental concept (Saussure).

Signifier: The sound/material aspect of communication (Saussure).

Sign: Saussure's system of describing the triad of signifier, signified, sign.

Simulcra: Baudrillard's designation of cultural sign systems that present an appearance as reality. Evolving historically, simulcra are categories that determine how a culture understands itself and its institutions.

Social self-formation: Active doing, passive-undergoing activity of creating self and being created by the culture. Language acquisition and language use are the prime examples.

Structuralism: Saussure's model of language as a sign system built on binary relationships of difference.

Subjectivity: The self for poststructuralists; a language construction.

Supplement: Derrida's term identifying the marginal hidden device that fills a lack in the primary term of an argument and simultaneously overturns a final, authoritative interpretation.

Symbolic Order: In the largest sense, that which comprises all of the signs (linguistic, institutional, etc.) that represent the culture. In Lacan, the child's resolution of the Oedipal Conflict, signaled by the child's acquisition of language and identity.

Syntagm: The logically ordered collection of signs; John is a man.

Transcendental Signifier: Derrida's term to identify a term having the qualities of a metaphysical self-presence, i.e., apartheid.

Index

A

Abernaty, Ralph, 40
abject, 159, 162, 167
absolute subject, 44
Afro-American, 31, 81, 143
Afrocentric, 125, 132-134,140, 171
Afrocentricity, xiv, 31-34, 40-43
Afrocentrist, 36, 130, 140
Afro-American, 125, 130
alienation, 20, 35, 36, 46, 102
Althusser, Louis, xii, xiv, 30-32, 34, 36-39, 43-45, 47
American Common School, xiv
American Creed, 48, 127-128, 136-138
American Dream, xiv, 48, 53, 58
anti-Semite, 119, 121
apartheid, 112, 113, 115
archeology, 75
Aristotle, 2
Asante, Molefi Kate, xiv, 30-34, 38, 40-42, 46
attention, 6

B

Barhtes, Roland, xii, xiv, xv, xvi, 47-51, 61, 62, 72, 73, 159, 163-166, 172
Baudrillard, Jean, xii, xv, 89-94, 96, 105, 172
behavior, 8
Bernstein, Richard J., 21
bliss, 159
body, 8, 13

bricolage, 172
bricoleur, xiii
Brown v. Board Education of Topeka (1954), 31

C

California Reading Readiness Test, xv, 74, 79, 80, 82-88
Capitalism, 23, 36, 40
Capitalist, 126
categorical attitude, 13
Cézanne, Paul, xii, 3, 10, 11, 13, 14
chiasm, xiii, 12, 46
Christie, Agatha, 166
cogito, 96
commodity, 27, 92-94
commodity fetishism, 26, 71, 72
Common School, 52
connotation, xiv
consciousness, 2
Cubberly, Ellwood, xiv, 48, 55, 56, 59
cultural myth, xiv
cultural pluralism, 122-125, 127, 128, 134, 141,143

D

Deconstruction, xii, 143, 172
desire, 29
denotation, xiv
Derrida, Jacques, xii, xv, xvi, 2, 105, 106-118, 135, 143, 150, 172-173
de Sade, 166
Dewey, John, xiv, xv, 16-18, 22-25, 27-29, 59-69, 71, 72, 90, 91, 94, 96-102, 106, 171, 172
différance, xiv, xv, xvi, 1, 2, 106, 107, 111, 116, 135, 150, 151
discourse, 74, 78
discursive practices, xi
Disneyland, 92, 95
Douglass, Frederick, 134, 142
Dubois, W.E.B., 41, 134, 142
Duras, Marguerite, xvi, 159, 167, 168

X

Z

ERUPTIONS
New Thinking across the Disciplines

Erica McWilliam
General Editor

This is a series of red-hot women's writing after the "isms." It focuses on new cultural assemblages that are emerging from the de-formation, breakot   minism. The
series brings   ien's writing
that, while sti   **DATE DUE**   s not rely on
neat disciplin   This writing
transcends sc   es of a first
generation of   has come to
terms with i   matory, and
ungovernable.

The aim c   more readily
available to u   iers and new
academics, a   is, we seek
contributions   expressed in
texts that are   lership.

Proposals   ns of: "post"
humanities, I   idies, literary
criticism, info   arts, gay and
lesbian studi   jogics, social
psychology, i   interested in
publishing re: om Australia,
New Zealand

For furth   submission of
manuscripts,   GAYLORD   #3522PI   Printed in USA

Queensland University of Technology
Victoria Park Rd., Kelvin Grove Q 4059
Australia

To order other books in this series, please contact our Customer Service Department at:

(800) 770-LANG (within the U.S.)
(212) 647-7706 (outside the U.S.)
(212) 647-7707 FAX

Or browse online by series at:

www.peterlangusa.com